INCOMING

INCOMING

On the Front Lines of
the Left's War on Truth

BIANCA DE LA GARZA

Post Hill
PRESS

A POST HILL PRESS BOOK
ISBN: 979-8-88845-806-8
ISBN (eBook): 979-8-88845-807-5

Incoming:
On the Front Lines of the Left's War on Truth
© 2024 by Bianca de la Garza
All Rights Reserved

Cover photo by Maarten de Boer Photography
Cover design by Conroy Accord

Post Hill Press
New York • Nashville
posthillpress.com

Published in the United States of America
1 2 3 4 5 6 7 8 9 10

For my daughter. Giving you life gave me life.

TABLE OF CONTENTS

CHAPTER ONE

THE LEGACY
MEDIA LION'S DEN

You never forget your first time.

As I stepped through the front door of the Washington Hilton, I could tell right away that I was in the wrong place. There, standing in the middle of the nondescript lobby, was a scene right out of a nightmare: hundreds of members of the corporate media and Hollywood elite, all rubbing shoulders and shaking hands, flashing their fake smiles, and trying not to let their Botox show under the dim, flickering lights.

For a moment, I froze.

The primal part of my brain—the one that lights up in dark parking garages at night, alerting women to the presence of creeps and con-men and predators—told me to kick off my heels and run away.

Get out of here, Bianca, it said. *Go find some normal people to hang out with tonight. There's still time!*

Already, I had endured a few unexpected detours. Outside the hotel, there was an unruly crowd of angry Hamas supporters, their heads covered with keffiyeh, some with their hands and faces covered in red paint. As I walked past them toward the front door, they'd screamed, "Shame on you!" "Free Palestine!" and other ignorant chants. Even now, over the muted conversation and dull music, I could still hear the bullhorns. So, turning back wasn't really an option. It's not like I was going to risk getting a big red handprint on my dress.

I pressed on.

It was April 2024, and the White House Correspondents' Dinner was about to begin.

Over the years, I'd watched a few of these dinners on television. They'd looked about as appealing to me as a night in a crack house with Hunter Biden. So, I'd never gotten too bent out of shape about not being invited, even after more than three decades in the journalism business.

Still, when I was invited to "nerd prom," as it's called around the Beltway, I decided to give it a shot. Early in my career as a reporter, I learned that seeing something with your own eyes is always better than seeing it through the lens or filter of someone else. There was no substitute for getting out, pounding the pavement, and seeing what something was really like. Over the years, that impulse had led me to the scenes of countless SWAT standoffs, police chases, and murder scenes. It had brought me within spitting distance of serious danger, and it had also allowed me to land some of the most memorable scoops of my career.

Now, it was going to lead me straight through this crowd of Trump haters and swamp creatures—right into the lion's den.

Moving through the lobby, I was curious and excited. Familiar faces floated by in the distance, all headed toward the cavernous ballroom at the hotel's center, where tables of ten and twelve were arranged and set for dinner. I was happy to see that my dress, a vintage black caftan, helped me blend in with the crowd. A few days earlier, when I was still considering the invitation, I'd asked a friend who'd been to a few of the dinners over the years what I should wear.

"Don't go overboard, Bianca," he'd said. "DC thinks Laura Ashley is haute couture."

At the time, I'd been holding a red satin gown in front of my face on a hanger, deciding whether I could get it dry-cleaned in time for the dinner. I'd laughed, throwing it down on my bed, and decided to go with my black caftan, which had a V-neck and pearls running up the collar. I figured it was Jackie O with a slight Arabian flair. Or, as my colleagues in this room might call it: cultural appropriation.

Now, even that was beginning to seem like too much. Women milled around their white-clothed tables in outfits of black and navy. I found my seat at the Newsmax table, champagne flute in hand, and scanned the faces in the gathering crowd.

Senator Chuck Schumer, whom I covered decades ago during my first years as a cub reporter in Albany, was there. So were Secretary of the Treasury Janet Yellen and Jeffrey Katzenberg, co-chair of Joe Biden's reelection campaign. I had to admit, as a journalist, that being close to power felt good. As a young reporter, I used to hang around the halls of state capitals, microphone in hand, just to get a brush-off quote from people like this. Now twenty-five years later, while I was often interviewing and covering stories about the politicians in the room, I rarely found myself in social situations with them.

That's because I wasn't one of them.

Far from it.

I grew up working class in a small Boston suburb. My single mother worked as a flight attendant to put me through school, and she taught me that the only way to get ahead in life was by working hard (and looking good while you did it). I rose through the ranks of TV journalism without a single connection, more or less annoying my way to the top by refusing to take no for an answer. An approach I now call "pleasantly persistent." Using my mother's work ethic and my own brand of hard-nosed reporting, I earned my right to spend three hours a day talking straight to the American people as an anchor on Newsmax, one of the few media outlets that hasn't gone completely insane over the past few years.

Unlike some of my colleagues gathered in the Washington Hilton that evening, I didn't have to lie to my audience. I didn't have to pretend that people could change genders at the drop of a hat, or that the campus protestors chanting for the murder of Jews were just a bunch of young rascals out having a good time. I definitely didn't have to pretend, as they all did, that Joe Biden was anything other than an old man with serious cognitive issues.

Not that my conscience would have allowed me to do so anyway.

By the night of the dinner, I had watched the Biden crew implement the most inflationary policies this country had ever seen. Food was more expensive. Gasoline was more expensive. Even red wine—which, for some, was an absolute necessity if you were going to watch the news in Joe Biden's America—was more expensive. Not to mention that World War III seemed imminent. Every morning, I woke up and checked my phone to find news of some new thing for my viewers to freak out about. Russia, emboldened by our nation's weak commander in chief, had made credible threats of nuclear strikes. Iran had already sent dozens of missiles into Israel, presumably purchased with the $10 billion that Team Biden had allowed the regime to access in the form of relief from sanctions—a complete reversal of the Trump administration's policies.

The Middle East was in shambles. Small-town America wasn't doing much better. And all Joe Biden seemed concerned about was keeping his radical, left-wing base happy. On the rare occasions he managed to string a full sentence together, that sentence usually had something to do with "ultra-MAGA Republicans" (by which he meant the sizeable percentage of the electorate who still supported Donald Trump). Rather than being tough on Hamas, an *actual terror group*, the Biden administration had decided to go all-in on prosecuting people who'd participated peacefully in protests on January 6, 2021, handing out sentences with "terrorism enhancements" that put them away for years. And rather than trying to beat former President Trump on his record—which included no new wars, a booming economy, and a president who knew where he was and didn't need to wear diapers—Joe Biden's administration had put him on trial for nonsensical crimes, putting the United States on a fast track to becoming a third-world banana republic. All the while, they insisted that it was Donald Trump, the candidate who did *not* routinely try to lock up his political opponents, who posed the threat of "fascism." If George Orwell, patron saint of journalists everywhere, watched one of these programs for more than five minutes, he'd probably run screaming.

When the anchors of CNN, MSNBC, and other legacy media networks accidentally stumbled on these facts, they tended to pretend they weren't real. Or blame Donald Trump. Whatever was easier. When the *New York Times* got wind that people were concerned about rising crime rates, it published a piece insisting that crime was not, in fact, rising, and that anyone who thought so was a right-wing racist. When CNBC heard that people were concerned about rampant inflation, it published an article titled "The Economy Is Doing Well; Why Don't Americans Know It?" insisting that the high prices (which *everyone* had seen with their own eyes) were just an illusion that stupid people believed.

Even the supposedly objective news outlets that I had grown up with no longer believed in their mission as brokers of the truth. Instead, they saw their role in society as defeating "racism," "fascism," and "white supremacy." They would twist any fact if it meant helping Joe Biden and hurting Donald Trump.

Even if they had to lie. Blatantly.

The attitude of the mainstream media had been summed up by Katherine Maher, the clown-like figure who'd recently been appointed CEO of NPR, during a TED talk she gave in 2012: "For most of our tricky disagreements," she said, "seeking the truth and seeking to convince others of the truth might not be the right place to start. In fact, our reverence for the truth might be a distraction that's getting in the way of finding common ground and getting things done."

Which brings me to the most important difference between me and the hundreds of so-called journalists gathered in the Washington Hilton ballroom that evening: I still did my job, and I still cared about the truth. When I saw inflation, I called it inflation. When I saw a doddering old man step up to the podium in the White House briefing room, I called him that (or whatever my producers would let me get away with). In my mind, the proper relationship between a journalist and a politician, to quote the great journalist H. L. Mencken, "should be akin to that between a dog and a lamppost."

In other words, I wanted to report on people in power, not suck up to them at fancy dinners and Ivy League alumni events (not that I got invited to many of those anyway). I wanted to work in a journalism industry that was much more like the one I'd grown up in: irreverent, fun, and staffed by people who could take a joke. More than anything, I wanted to seek the truth, not push a narrative. Luckily, there were a few journalists left in the world who agreed with me. Most of them were gathered around the Newsmax table with smiles on their faces, laughing rather than looking around for things at which to take offense. At *this* table, where the cool kids sat, you could say things that were forbidden pretty much everywhere else in the room. You could, for instance, openly declare that there were only two genders, or that hairy men with penises shouldn't be allowed into locker rooms with little girls. You could say that most people probably didn't need to get forty-seven COVID-19 booster shots. You could even say "make America great again," as long as you did it under your breath and out of sight of the security cameras.

Anywhere else in the room, that kind of talk would get you in big trouble. Say any of that at the MSNBC table, and someone was bound to start crying. Say it at the NPR table, and one of the journalists would probably file federal hate crime charges and put on a neck brace. Somehow, the profession I had loved for so many years had become filled with a bunch of whiny, miseducated babies, always ready to pounce on one another for saying the wrong thing or expressing the wrong opinion. If *I* were working at one of these classic outlets, I might have been scared. After all, I have more "wrong opinions" than a wild dog has fleas.

By choice, I wasn't working for the legacy media. I was an actual journalist, here in the Hall of Propaganda as a representative of one of the last networks in the country willing to call out those in power and report the facts.

After standing around and talking with my colleagues for a few minutes, cracking jokes and dodging frosty glares from the mainstream reporters in the room, I decided to branch out a little. I mean, what's the point of going to the zoo if you're not going to check out the reptile cage, right?

As I ventured out, some of the other advice my friend had given me rang in my head. *Bring mints, Bianca. Eat before you get there, because the food is bad. Don't drink too much at dinner.* And, most important: *Work the room. If there's someone you want to cultivate as a source—and there will be—put your phone in their hand and get their contact info. Don't be shy.*

I had to chuckle at that last one.

Over the course of my career, people have called me many things, some of which aren't fit to print here.

"Shy" isn't one of them.

Right away, I bumped into Alejandro Mayorkas, Joe Biden's head of the Department of Homeland Security. I couldn't help but wince because, due to this man's disastrous dereliction of duty, the DHS had allowed border crossings to surge to levels that were previously unthinkable. For years on my show at Newsmax—*Newsline*—I had been exposing the full-blown crisis he and his boss had created, from the horror of children who'd been found abandoned in the desert, and the eighty-five thousand children lost across America, to the trafficked women who've been raped and exploited by drug cartels in the wake of Biden's wide open border policy.

I wanted to interview this guy. Or at least ask him how he slept at night (although I suspected the answer was: *upside down, in a cave, with the other nocturnal monsters*). So, I swallowed my disgust, walked right up to him, and asked him to come on my show. He agreed immediately, with the canned response, *Have your people call my people.*

And then I was off, walking into another sea of famous faces. One of them, which sat a little below the rest, belonged to Dr. Anthony Fauci, quite possibly the most disastrous public servant in the history of the United States. He waved at me (probably mistaking me for somebody else), and I had to acknowledge him while thinking of all the businessowners who'd had their life's work destroyed because of his horrible lockdown policies. I thought of all the people who'd been forced to watch loved ones die through plastic barriers because of his six-feet-apart rule (which would later be revealed to have been based on nothing).

Interview questions flooded my mind, as they often did after so many years as a reporter.

Research now shows that COVID-19 began in a laboratory in Wuhan, a possibility you have dismissed. Why did you lie to the American people?

Do you feel any responsibility for the thousands of deaths of despair—suicide, overdoses, and others—that your lockdowns caused? Will you apologize?

Instead of saying that, though, I smiled, unable to break through the crowd of admirers (most of whom were journalists) eager to shake Dr. Fauci's hand and get a selfie with him.

He smiled back, and my creep senses kicked in again.

From there, I worked the room, just like my friend had told me to do. Everywhere I walked, there was someone whose politics I abhorred. Congresswoman Rashida Tlaib, for instance, stood far away in the middle of a crowd. I saw a few members of the White House press corps—who, unbeknownst to the American people, were suppressing stories that very night about the true condition of Joe Biden behind the scenes—and brushed past them.

After a few more brief conversations, the lights dimmed. People began walking to their tables. I nabbed a few more phone numbers and headed back to my seat, settling in for a long night.

The crowd went quiet as the guests of honor took the stage. Out came Vice President Kamala Harris and her husband Doug, followed by "Dr." Jill Biden and the president, who surprised us all by finding his chair without bumping into anything on the way. There were a few short speeches to kick things off, along with some remarks about the amazing power of journalism to—I don't know, *guard the sacred flame of democracy* or something?

To be honest, I stopped listening after about an hour, and I began scanning the faces in the crowd, trying and failing to calculate exactly how much damage these people had done to my country over the years. Whether it was the Democrat members of Congress who'd enriched themselves while failing the American people, or the useless journalists of the mainstream media who continually covered for them, I couldn't help feeling angry on behalf of the people I'd grown up around—honest, hardworking citizens who wanted to provide for their families, and be told the truth when they turned on their televisions at night.

Around hour two, Colin Jost of *Saturday Night Live* took to the stage for the evening's main event. I was surprised by his willingness to go after Joe Biden's age at the same time as he was cracking jokes about President Trump's indictments. The routine was funnier than I'd expected. As the program went on, I kept scanning the room. There was Joe Biden, beginning to nod off. Just a few feet away, Kamala Harris sat cackling at all the jokes. Just a few months into the future, after a disastrous debate performance and some backroom maneuvering on the part of the Democrat elite, Laffin' Kamala would find herself at the top of the ticket, accompanied by a governor from the Midwest named Tim Walz—who, at the time, was famous for presiding over the disastrous George Floyd protests that destroyed Minneapolis during the summer of 2020. And just like that, everyone in this room—who, at the time, was telling us that Joe Biden was "the best he's ever been" and "sharper than ever"—would get their new talking points, beginning to tell us that Kamala was the greatest person ever to run for the White House. At least five of them would write long magazine pieces about whether Kamala was having a "brat summer" (whatever that means).

In the final hundred days before the 2024 election, the media elite with whom I was rubbing shoulders on the night of the Correspondents' Dinner would completely forget that Kamala Harris, who had to drop out of the presidential primary before a single vote was cast, seemed to have no real political skills. They would get together and pretend that she had never uttered some of her most ridiculous lines—such as "more police make us less safe" or "it's time for us to do what we have been doing, and that time is every day." These people expected us to forget that Kamala had slept her way to the top of her profession, and that she did not seem to know how an English sentence works.

As Colin Jost wrapped up, I found myself thinking of President Ronald Reagan, who was shot while leaving this very hotel in 1981. I wondered what it must have been like for Americans to get news that the president of the United States was being rushed to the hospital after a crazed gunman attempted to take his life.

Soon, I would find out exactly what that was like.

For now, I was still in the legacy media lion's den, looking around for potential interview subjects and marveling at the big names around me. Earlier in the evening, I had hoped that attending this dinner would give me a sense of camaraderie with my fellow journalists—like a high school prom where we all hung out and danced and forgot our troubles. For a few hours after the party, it did.

But as the election cycle wore on in the months that followed, I found myself more and more disgusted at the way our media was blatantly lying to the American people. I grew even more disenchanted with the legacy media every day as I watched them hurl baseless lies at President Trump. At an afterparty of the White House Correspondents' Dinner, I met a reporter from *Time* magazine who'd just written a balanced, non-ideological profile of the forty-fifth president. I remember thinking that night about how nice it was to have at least one magazine that still believed in covering things accurately. Little did I know that just a few months later, in the aftermath of an assassination attempt on President Trump, *Time* would refuse to use the famous photograph of him raising his fist on its cover, believing that it "made him look too good."

Today, there are almost no journalists left who don't adhere to the Democrat Party line. And it's no wonder. These days, anyone who doesn't fall in line is smeared as a racist and a fascist. As the radical Left loses control of the public, it holds even tighter to the institutions that it does control, primarily the media. As a result, too many Americans are brainwashed into believing lies.

Over the next couple hundred pages, I'll go through all the ways in which the Left has taken control of America's institutions, and I'll expose the lies that it told to do so. Unlike most of today's journalists, I'll do it using facts and original reporting. Along the way, I'll include some of the best interviews I've conducted during my time as the host of *Newsline*. I'll also tell a few stories about my career, which spans almost thirty years and several cities around the country. We'll travel to the halls of the state capital in Albany, New York, where I got my start, dip down to our nation's southern border where I can compare illegal crossings from twenty years ago with today's invasion, and bring it all home to the free state of Florida, where many of our nation's most important culture wars are being fought. It also happens to be the location of Mar-a-Lago—the place where Donald Trump reigns, and the FBI raids.

So, turn the page, and let's get rolling.

CHAPTER TWO

THE AMERICAN DREAM

"Don't come back without the story, kid."
I was already halfway out the door, a reporter's note-book in my hand, when Don Decker called out to me. Every time I left the newsroom, he'd give me this line.

And he meant it.

More than anything else, Don demanded excellence. When you handed him a story, that story needed to be flaw-less. If it wasn't, he'd come over and smack your desk with his cane while letting you know what you'd done wrong. But he had a heart of gold, and he wanted every one of his reporters to succeed.

I told him I was on it.

A few minutes later, my photographer and I were standing at the front door of a suspected criminal. Although I don't remember precise details, I do remember that I wanted to get this guy's picture. *Bad.* Best case scenario, I'd get an exclusive interview with him—maybe even a full confession. (Unlikely, but I tended to dream big back then.)

I knocked three times, giving my photographer the signal to be ready.

No answer.

The photographer and I looked at one another. Here we were, standing in a rough part of town with only a shoulder-mounted news camera and a microphone to ward off would-be assailants. I thought about shrugging my shoulders and heading home. It was the sensible thing for a five-foot-six woman in four-inch heels to do.

But Don's words rang in my ears.

Don't come back without the story.

For the past few months, I'd been trying like hell to prove myself. Don Decker, a veteran newsman in the Albany area, had taken a big chance hiring me before I was even done with college. I wanted to show him that he hadn't made a mistake by giving me my big break.

I walked a few steps to the left and peered around the back of the house. Technically, it's trespassing if you stay on personal property. But just walking around and knocking is well within the bounds of legality. I'd learned that in school, then again during my on-the-job training as an unpaid intern at Cablevision News in Brockton, Massachusetts, where I'd worked for eight months in the mid-'90s. But no one had said anything to me about *knocking* repetitively on the back door.

I gave my photographer another signal, and he gave me one back: a wide-eyed, mouth-agape look that seemed to mean, *Are you out of your mind?*

Which I was. Back then, I'd have done anything to get the story. We crept along the side of the house, checking the windows for signs of the suspect, and landed at the creaky back door. Cigarette butts littered the ground around me. The lawn was dirty and overgrown. I could have sworn I heard growling from behind the rusted-out screen door.

I knocked again, a little harder this time, and backed up.

And out came one of the largest, angriest dogs I have ever seen in my life, more like a creature out of a Stephen King movie than anything I had ever seen strolling along a sidewalk on a leash. The dog snapped its teeth and let loose giant ropes of slobber, snarling like mad as it chased me and my photographer back out to our car. In my mind, we made it just in time to hop headfirst into the van and shut the door behind us, thanking God the angry beast wasn't a fast runner.

Later that evening, I came back to the newsroom with a story—just not the one Don and the rest of the team had been counting on me to get. To this day, that dog chase sticks in my memory not just because it was crazy and dangerous (which it was), but because it was one of the rare nights when I came back to the station empty handed. During that first year on the job as a reporter, my tactics out in the field got me whatever quote or scoop I'd gone out looking for. I was hungrier than a '90s waif model surviving on cigarettes and coffee (but definitely less rich). For me, the job was not about the money. It was about getting the truth. I worked long hours, chased down every lead, and put work before my social life, all to get ahead in my profession.

In recent years, I've found myself wondering how many young journalists would have gone around the back door and taken their chances with Cujo just to get the story. I wonder how many would have kicked off their heels and chased a suspect down a snow-lined street in the middle of winter.

Looking around the industry lately, I suspect the answer is *not many*.

For those of you who were raised to believe that hard work and going the extra mile were virtues, allow me to give you a quick primer on the lazy-and-proud ethos of Gen Z.

According to *Business Insider*, the "quiet quitting" trend went viral in July 2022, when the aptly named TikTok user @zchillin defined it in a video as "not outright quitting your job, but quitting the idea of going above and beyond. You're still performing your duties, but you're no longer subscribing to the hustle culture mentality that work has to be your life."[1] That video was seen over three million times, and more than 150 million people liked it.

In its wake, hundreds of thousands more followed. One user, sitting in the driver's seat of his car, said, "I'm not going to put in a sixty-hour workweek and pull myself up by my boot-straps for a job that does not care about me as a person." In the words of Adam Grant, a writer who purports to speak for the young generation: "'Quiet quitting' isn't laziness. Doing the bare minimum is a common response to bullshit jobs, abusive bosses, and low pay. When they don't feel cared about, people eventually stop caring."[2] Clearly, this up-and-coming generation has problems. They expect their employers to *care* about them and cater to their needs, just like their parents have done since they were babies. Rather than showing up to the office every day trying to do excellent work, they stay home in their pajamas, performing only the tasks necessary to avoid getting fired.

You might think that this is just an isolated phenomenon, common only to a few underachieving TikTok influencers. But it's not. According to a Gallup poll conducted in September 2022, the number of people who "do the minimum required and are psychologically detached from their job" describes "half of the U.S. workforce."[3] The largest group

1 Harriet Marsden, "TikTok is credited with coining the term 'quiet quitting.' Now it's turned against it," *Business Insider*, October 3, 2022, https://www. businessinsider.com/tiktok-coined-the-term-quiet-quitting-now-its-turned-against-it-2022-9 (accessed September 2, 2024).

2 Adam Grant, "'Quiet quitting' isn't laziness…." X, August 26, 2022, https:// x.com/AdamMGrant/status/1563164741987893248 (accessed September 2, 2024).

3 Jim Harter, "Is Quiet Quitting Real?" Gallup, September 6, 2022, updated May 17, 2023, https://www.gallup.com/workplace/398306/quiet-quitting-real.aspx#:~:text=Many%20quiet%20quitters%20fit%20Gallup's,or%20actively%20disengaged%20(18%25) (accessed September 18, 2024).

of those who report being "not engaged" at work are, unsurprisingly, those born after 1989.

In my profession, you can't afford to be lazy. Finding the truth isn't something that people can do by mindlessly scrolling social media while sipping oat milk lattes. But I worry that with the advent of artificial intelligence programs like ChatGPT, this problem will only get worse. Now, rather than sitting up with public records and poring over documents the way my colleagues and I had to do in the early stages of investigative pieces, young reporters will simply rely on some AI chatbot to handle the heavy lift for them. And if they get caught, they'll probably just call their helicopter parents, some of whom have been there for the past twenty years to clean up all the messes they've made. With AI, their new enabler, I have a hard time believing that *any* of them would go the extra mile the way my friends and I had to when we first got started.

My first job in journalism sometimes required me to go out in rough neighborhoods and talk to complete strangers to get the story. I engaged with people from all walks of life, often giving a voice to the voiceless. Sometimes I encountered aggression. I have been shoved and spit on. I was an adrenaline junkie (still am), and the journalism profession fed my need for the rush. The deadlines, the long hours, and the intensity from landing at a scene with mere minutes to deduce what was going on gave me a thrill I just couldn't get anywhere else. My colleagues and I loved the idea that we might break the next big story. Putting in extra hours at the office was *fun* for us.

I can't imagine some of the reporters who are coming up today—so many of whom have been educated at elite universities—doing that kind of dirty work. You might remember that in the summer of 2020, shortly after the *New York Times* ran an op-ed by Senator Tom Cotton calling for President Trump to "send in the troops" to quell the riots that were then reducing our cities to wastelands out of a *Mad Max* movie,

Times staffers began tweeting that the op-ed *literally* put them in danger. I can only imagine what any of these people would do when faced with real trouble out in the field.

Not that they ever actually get out there.

This kind of apathy has consequences. It allows elite media institutions to create a false picture of what this country really looks like. It allows them to distort and misrepresent what people think—to flatten the "flyover states" (as they call them) into big open spaces filled with MAGA-loving racists, all while portraying the crime-infested cities where *they* live as paragons of love and tolerance. If you ever wonder why anchors on CNN were so surprised when Donald Trump won the presidential election in November 2016, *this* is why. Their reporters didn't talk to anyone. No one did the work! They just assumed that what their friends had been telling them at cocktail parties was correct, and they filed their stories accordingly.

Today, things are different. With nearly *half* the workforce meeting the Gallup poll definition of "quiet quitter," the phenomenon has likely spread everywhere. I'm sure that when Elon Musk arrived at the headquarters of Twitter, which he bought in October 2022, he learned just how true this was. There, in the middle of San Francisco, he found a staff of about 7,500 that included, in his words, "a lot of people doing things that didn't seem to have a lot of value." So, he fired about half of them, and the site continued to run despite the drastic reduction in forces. A few weeks later, he sent an email to the full staff, letting them know that "long hours and intense dedication" would be required to turn the company around. Another 1,500 employees—most of them young people who vented their frustrations on social media—quit. Apparently, having no job at all was better than having a job that required them to work hard. In the months that followed, another five hundred or so staffers left the company, bringing the headcount down to a little over one thousand—a mere

20 percent of what Musk found when he first entered Twitter headquarters.

So far, things are going swimmingly without them.

As Elon Musk told Tucker Carlson in April 2023, "If you don't care about censorship, you don't need a lot of people running Twitter."[4] As of this writing, the platform, now named X, is still running smoothly, and the lack of those six thousand staffers hasn't changed things one bit (other than to increase freedom of speech and reduce censorship). Aside from being kind of funny, this example demonstrates one of the biggest problems with doing the bare minimum at your job: Eventually, someone is going to fire you. It might not be Elon Musk walking into the building with a kitchen sink and a laptop. But it'll be someone.

And even if you don't get fired, doing the bare minimum is no way to go through life. In my opinion, coasting is a crime. For one thing, it degrades your spirit. Waking up every day and half-assing something you hate will not bring you nearly as much joy as whole-assing something you love. Or, at the very least, something that brings you fulfilment and a sense of purpose. Contrary to what many young people have been told all their lives, that thing does *not* necessarily entail four years at an expensive university. The world does not need more liberal arts grads who are fluent in transgender oppression studies with a concentration in DEI and LGBTQIA+ poetry. It doesn't need more kids who've been coddled into believing that they are supposed to follow their dreams and get degrees in things that will never make them any money. And it's about more than just career prospects. In this world, the way you do some things is how you do everything. If you're lazy at work,

---

4   Madeline Coggins, "Elon Musk knocks 'absurdly overstaffed' Twitter, 'desperate' media in Tucker Carlson sit-down," Fox News, April 18, 2023, https://www.foxnews.com/media/elon-musk-knocks-absurdly-overstaffed-twitter-desperate-media-tucker-carlson-sit-down (accessed September 2, 2024).

you're probably lazy at home, too. If you leave dishes in the sink and dirty socks on the floor, your mind is probably cluttered, too.

What the world needs more than anything is people with skills. *Real* skills. As in, the kind that people are willing to pay you money to use. According to a recent study conducted by a national staffing firm, there have been more than 770,000 skilled job postings from close to 100,000 different employers across the country since the beginning of 2023.[5] This country is in desperate need of plumbers, electricians, and construction workers. In his book *The Algebra of Wealth*, entrepreneur Scott Galloway points out that "the job market for electricians is projected to grow 40 percent faster than the overall job market" in the coming years; we're also projected to be "half a million plumbers short of what we will require by 2027. Yet only 17 percent of high school and college students are interested in pursuing the trades."[6]

Today, too many people—certainly those in the liberal bubbles of New York City and Washington, DC—look down on these careers. And yet when they can't get an electrician to hook up their new eco-friendly solar panels, they're the first to complain about it on Yelp. In recent years, the elites of this country have convinced their children that the only way to get ahead in life (or, more accurately, to signal status in an increasingly elite-centric world) is to go to a fancy university, take on a bunch of debt, and graduate four years later with a degree in some useless subject that barely fits on the diploma.

I'm telling you that it's not. The way to get ahead in life is to identify what you do better than most people, and to get very good at doing it. I discovered relatively early that my

---

5   Citation from author notes.

6   Scott Galloway, *The Algebra of Wealth: A Simple Formula for Financial Security* (New York: Portfolio, 2024), p. 89.

God-given talent happened to be chasing down stories and reporting them in a way that people wanted to watch. I haven't always loved every minute of doing it, but I've always felt that it was the thing I'm supposed to spend my life doing. If you think hard enough, I *know* you have one, too. And it might not be the thing you think it is (or the thing you hope it is). But the more you do it, the more you'll grow to love it, especially if people are giving you money to do it, and you're using that money to support your family. During my childhood, I watched my mother go to work every day to support me, and she was one of the happiest people I ever knew. The same went for friends of my parents who worked in factories, stores, and doctors' offices around town.

They knew that it was hard work, not instant gratification, that brought true fulfillment. They understood that the Declaration of Independence mentioned the *pursuit* of happiness for a reason—because it is the pursuit of happiness, not the attainment of it, that really counts. Hard work isn't just good for your boss and for the economy; it's good for you, too, physically, emotionally, and spiritually.

Too many young people are not getting this message, and it's setting them up for failure. In 2022, according to the Federal Reserve Bank of St. Louis, more than a third of people between the ages of eighteen and twenty-four reported no income from wages or a salary. That's up from just 22 percent in 1990, when I got my first job at the age of fifteen—one that I would soon supplement with a second job to bring in some extra money so I could splurge on clothes and accessories, such as a favorite Swatch watch and Benneton sweater. At the time, hard work was all I'd ever known. I was taught this by my single mom and as soon as I could earn my own money, I wanted to give her a break.

For this generation, it's different. Many young people in their twenties still live at home, and they seem just fine with that arrangement. Last year, more than 40 percent of people in that age range said they would be fine dating someone who still lived with mom and dad. Weird, right? Oh wait, it gets worse. Half of them said they would turn down any job offer that did not offer the flexibility for remote work—that is, the ability to sit home at mom and dad's house, binging Netflix and doing a few Zoom calls every day to avoid getting fired. In one of the most troubling studies, one in ten members of this generation said they *never* intended to start working.

Clearly, we have a serious problem on our hands, and it's one we should have seen coming. For years, we've heard warnings that the coddling culture of parents combined with unchecked access to smartphones would lead to a generation that is unmotivated, overly sensitive, and unwell. Many people dismissed these warnings as alarmism. But everything that was predicted has come to pass—and more. As Jonathan Haidt has recently shown in his book *The Anxious Generation*, a combination of unchecked social media use and helicopter parenting has led to a generation that is more depressed and anxious than ever, with almost 25 percent self-reporting some serious mental disorder. Everything offends them. Throughout their lives, they've been coddled and catered to. Their parents watched their every move. When they got to college, all they had to do was organize a boycott, and the professors and administrators would cave to their outrageous demands.

Now that they're out in the world, they're expecting their employers to behave the same way. When Spotify announced that it would be acquiring the streaming rights to Joe Rogan's podcast, hundreds of employees staged a walkout at company headquarters because of Rogan's views on vaccines, just like they'd done back in college. When it didn't work, they demanded that Spotify include "content warnings" on controversial episodes of the podcast—meaning the ones that included accurate criticisms of the government's position on COVID-19. On that, they won. To this day, the "content warnings" are there, even on episodes that include things that later turned out to be true.

In newsrooms all over the country, employees stage union walkouts, demanding they be paid overtime for their lazy journalism. At book publishers, employees routinely stage protests when the company announces plans to publish "offensive" material. At the Hachette Book Group, the staff walked out and successfully pressured the company's leadership to cancel a memoir by Woody Allen. At Simon & Schuster, the staff walked out over a memoir by Vice President Mike Pence, although in that case, the bosses stood their ground and published the book anyway. The same happened when the publishing house announced a new book by Senator Josh Hawley.

One of the newest hot trends among young workers is "micro-feminism," which involves young women in the office "speaking about the small, everyday acts they're engaging in to clap back against sexism around the office."[7] If these workers would put as much effort into working as they put into concocting elaborate ways to *avoid* working, they'd probably all be running companies by now.

Instead, all they seem to want to do is skate by and find new things to be upset about.

It's no wonder that in a recent survey, 31 percent of managers filling entry-level positions said they actively avoid hiring members of Gen Z, and nearly all of the respondents (94 percent) "reported a Gen Z candidate acting inappropriately

---

7   Sarah Bregel, "Microfeminism: On TikTok, women share the little ways they fight sexism in the workplace," *Fast Company*, May 18, 2024, https://www. fastcompany.com/91125945/microfeminism-tiktok-trend-women-fight-ing-workplace-sexism (accessed September 18, 2024).

during an interview."[8] But you don't need to look at surveys to see that something is very wrong with this generation, as well as with older people who've adopted the young generation's values. All you have to do is open TikTok. In recent months, after so many years of talking about "quiet quitting," a new trend has emerged: This one is called "Quit-Tok," and it entails pretty much exactly what you'd think. Young people look straight into their phones and publicly condemn their employers, listing their grievances for all the world to hear—with their full names, and the names of their employers—and then quit.

In a TikTok video.

One of the young women who did this came to feel extreme regret about her decision. Speaking on Fox Business, she said she'd recently quit a job in the hospitality industry because she felt overworked and disrespected by her manager. So, she filmed a video in which she told off her boss publicly and announced her resignation.

"It seems like a cool way to show that you have power over others," she said, according to Fox. "But the next day I felt like it was stupid."[9]

Better late than never, I guess.

As these incidents pile up, it is becoming clearer every day that we are undergoing a spiritual crisis in this country. Young people no longer want to do the jobs that will sustain our economy in the long term. Many feel they are above these

8   Ginger Christ, "31% of hiring managers say they steer clear of Gen Z," HR Drive, January 29, 2024, https://www.hrdive.com/news/hiring-managers-steer-clear-of-gen-z/705571/ (accessed September 2, 2024).

9   Erica Lamberg, "'Quit-Tok' goes viral among younger workers as job experts caution against public pronouncements," Fox Business, April 4, 2024, https://www.foxbusiness.com/lifestyle/quit-tok-viral-younger-workers-job-experts-caution-public-pronouncements (accessed September 2, 2024).

jobs. As Mike Rowe, the former host of *Dirty Jobs*, put it a few years ago, "This is not just a skill gap, it is a *will* gap."[10]

I couldn't agree more.

When the highest aspiration of the new generation is to work remotely from their parents' house and quit as soon as things get rough, the American Dream is in trouble.

You might say we all *woke* up.

For now, the older generations can pick up the slack that the quiet quitters leave behind. They can answer the phone calls that come in before 10 a.m., which Gen Z believes should be "illegal." They can stay late to finish projects and go the extra mile when it's necessary, and they can speak with clients in person.

But that won't last forever. In my industry, we're already seeing what happens when a bunch of young, entitled people who know very little about the world are allowed to take over newsrooms. You get what Bari Weiss, a former opinion columnist at the *New York Times*, called "a kind of performance space," where "stories are chosen and told in a way to satisfy the narrowest of audiences, rather than to allow a curious public to read about the world and then draw their own conclusions." In her resignation letter from the *Times*, which should be required reading for all Americans, especially those interested in journalism, Weiss writes that "the paper of record is, more and more, the record of those living in a distant galaxy, one whose concerns are profoundly removed from the lives of most people. This is a galaxy in which, to choose a few recent examples, the Soviet space program is lauded for its 'diversity'; the doxing of teenagers in the name of justice

---

10 "Mike Rowe on the skills gap," Facebook, https://www.facebook.com/ FoxBusiness/videos/mike-rowe-on-the-skills-gap/324642201457821/ (accessed September 2, 2024).

is condoned; and the worst caste systems in human history includes the United States alongside Nazi Germany."

In other words: When journalists don't do the hard work of finding out what people think, they tend to assume everyone thinks like they do.

And lately, what they think is *insane*.

But that's just my neck of the woods. In other segments of the economy, who knows? What I *do* know is that ten years from now, I don't want to sit in the chair of a "quiet quitting" dentist and have him drop a drill in my mouth. I don't want to hire an accountant who's decided to "prioritize living a good life" rather than filing my taxes accurately, and wind up with the headache of an audit.

If we're going to have any hope of turning this country around, we need to come together and make some serious changes.

And we need to do it *now*.

~

Am I being a little too direct?

Sorry about that. Occupational hazard.

In truth, I know things aren't easy for young people today. Or anyone else, for that matter. In Joe Biden's America, it's harder than it's ever been to cover your monthly expenses, even with a good job that pays a decent salary. Given the fallout from the pandemic lockdowns and the sky-high inflation that resulted when our government decided to begin printing money out of nowhere, the economy is in shambles. So is everything else. I'm sure that if you're a young person beginning your career journey, it's easy to feel like you won't ever get ahead.

There's good reason for that. Today, according to Scott Galloway, "the median home price in the United States is six times the median annual income—fifty years ago it was two times—and the share of first-time buyers is barely half the historical average and the lowest on record. Marriage rates among all but the wealthiest cohort are down 15 percent since 1980, as people can't afford to tie the knot, much less have kids. Despite record growth in our broader prosperity, just 50 percent of Americans born in the 1980s are making more than their parents did at the same age, the lowest share ever."[11]

And then there's plain bad luck. Imagine, for a moment, what it's like to be a twenty-two-year-old getting out of college right now. Four years ago, your prom was probably canceled because of COVID-19. Then, when you got to college, you did most of it over Zoom. There were no parties, no chances to go out and connect with your peers. Then, when you *finally* thought you were going to get a break on graduation day, they cancelled it because a bunch of clowns in funny outfits decided to set up tents on the quad.

Life certainly hasn't been easy for young people.

Now, I don't say this to make excuses for the quiet quitters. I say it because any good journalist knows that getting both sides of the story—or at least a quote from someone who disagrees with you—is vital to reflecting reality.

But you know what? It hasn't been easy for anyone. Since the founding of the United States, every generation has had its challenges. In the days of Alexander Hamilton and John Adams, most people in the United States lived on a couple of dollars a year. Disease was rampant. Corsets probably weren't much fun, either.

But people lived through it. They lived through a civil war, a Great Depression, and two world wars, too. They did it because the American spirit is one of perseverance and hard work, not of coasting and trying to take the easy way out.

---

11   Galloway, *The Algebra of Wealth*, p. 5.

The hard work of previous generations is what has allowed for the creation of the amazing prosperity we enjoy today, and it is our duty not to squander it. To do that, we need to start looking up to people who embody the ideals that we used to hold sacred in this nation—not people who complain about how hard their lives are, but the ones who do amazing things *despite* how hard their lives are.

In the beginning of this chapter, I told you about my first news director, Don Decker. During the early years of my career in journalism, he was my mentor and taught me how to do the job well. Around the newsroom of WTEN, Don set the model for excellence, and we all followed it. He was the one who encouraged us to seek out all sides to a story, and to ensure that we weren't leaving a single scrap of information out. When we screwed up, he came down hard. But there was nothing like the feeling of getting something right for him.

On the day we met, I was still a senior at Emerson College. I'd driven all the way from Boston to Albany in my red Saab convertible, hitting every local television station I could find along the way to drop off my tape. When I walked into the offices of WTEN, I expected to get the same cold treatment I'd gotten everywhere else. Instead, the receptionist let me know that the news director was in.

Don Decker came walking out, supporting himself with a cane. He sat down with me in the TV station reception area and asked me questions about my life and my career aspirations. He even counseled me against taking a producing job that probably wouldn't be right for me. A few weeks later, he called me in for a formal interview. I spent the entire day there, was interviewed by key members of his staff, and as the day shift was ending, he offered me a job as a reporter and presented me with a two-year contract. I accepted, signing my contract before anyone could find out I hadn't even graduated college yet. Don Decker took a chance on me just like he'd taken chances on dozens of other broadcasters over his fifty years in the news business.

Over time, I learned Don's story. As a child, he'd battled polio, a disease that made it difficult for him to walk for the rest of his life. He wore leg braces and walked with a cane for most of his life. In high school, a teacher named Mrs. Rutherford noticed something special in Don and worked to get him into the journalism program at Syracuse University. From there, he worked day and night to acquire his skills, never allowing the pain from his disease to get in his way. By the time I arrived at WTEN in the late '90s, he had touched the lives of more local newscasters than I can count. When he died in 2012, many of them went on the record to talk about what he'd meant to their careers.

"He loved taking chances on people," said one. Another said he was "dedicated to the news business and the idea we should give the viewers good, fair, honest and thorough news coverage.... He was a throwback."

He was indeed.

Today, I believe we need to teach our children to look up to people like Don Decker—the ones who overcame seemingly insurmountable obstacles to achieve great things. Rather than demonizing hard work, we should venerate it. And rather than simply accepting a media that gets all its material straight from the Biden White House or the Harris campaign, we should look to journalists who came up doing the hard work that allowed American journalism to thrive.

That means following good journalists who actually get out and talk to Americans, rather than sitting on their computers and typing up bad opinion pieces dressed up as news. It means learning what the Left has done to our media and beginning to recognize state propaganda when we see it. Luckily, I've reported extensively on the ways the Left has corrupted our education system—a system that today's young woke journalists have all gone through, learning all the nonsense words like "intersectionality" and "oppression" that Kamala Harris and Co. slip into their press releases every day.

And although it might get crazy, I'm happy to take you to school, too.

So, grab your pencil case and your state-issued copies of *Gender Queer* and *Antiracist Baby*.

Class begins now.

CHAPTER THREE

FROM EDUCATION TO INDOCTRINATION

S ince we're going to be talking about school for the next few pages, we might as well begin with a pop quiz.

1. *Have you, at some point over the past few days, shown up to an appointment on time?*

2. *Do you value hard work?*

3. *Do you like books?*

Well, I hate to break it to you, but if you answered "yes" to any of the above, you might be a white supremacist—at least in the eyes of your local school board.

According to a presentation that has been used to train teachers all over the country, concepts such as "following rigid time schedules," "believing that hard work is the key to success," and "worship of the written word" are all racist.[1] Teachers who insist that their students do any of these things—especially work hard—are simply reinforcing "white supremacy culture."

---

1   Robby Soave, "Educators, Please Stop Teaching the Characteristics of 'White Supremacy Culture,'" *Reason*, February 4, 2022, https://reason.com/2022/02/04/characteristics-of-white-supremacy-culture-washington-university/ (accessed September 3, 2024).

And these teachers don't even have to be white! Ridiculously, Latinos and blacks can also qualify for the white supremacist label. According to a recent article in *The New Yorker*, it is possible to be "a Latino white supremacist." When Larry Elder was running for governor of California, his hometown newspaper, the *Los Angeles Times*, called him "the black face of white supremacy" because he dared to support conservative values. Things sure have changed since my youth.

When I was in elementary school, my peers and I had to be good students. We were expected to show up on time, behave in class, ask for permission to leave, and respect our elders. Those Catholic nuns at St. Agatha's in East Milton, Massachusetts, did not mess around. We also tended to learn from books. (Imagine that.) For the next few decades, even as my daughter made her way through middle and high school in the mid-2010s, I assumed that those basic rules hadn't changed. I checked over her homework when she was young, finding math that looked somewhat familiar to me. I attended parent-teacher conferences dutifully and never detected anything too strange. Like millions of other parents, I figured that school was still about preparing children to go out into the world.

Educating them, in other words.

Then COVID-19 hit, and kids all began doing their classes over Zoom. Now, rather than getting updates every few weeks in the form of report cards, parents saw exactly what went on in the classrooms of their children.

And often, what they saw was *not* education.

It was indoctrination.

During those early months of the pandemic, as far-left governors all over the country refused to allow schools and businesses to reopen, parents got a good look at some of the nonsense being spoon-fed to their children every day. We overheard Zoom calls about "oppression" and "systemic racism" and "spirit murder" (which, for those of you lucky enough not to have encountered this nonsense, is defined as "the practice by which children of color are made to feel *less than* or *othered* by educators enforcing white supremacist ideals"). We listened while teachers recited strange lines about gender and sexuality to young children. Online, communities of concerned parents came together and began sharing all the things they were seeing on the screens of their children's iPads and laptops.

Even for me, whose job, at least in part, it is to cover the dangers of the woke Left, the stuff was shocking. Every story I read disturbed me more than the last one. In California, for instance, white children in elementary school were forced to sit on the ground with their heads down while "children of color" screamed at them. When teachers were questioned about this barbaric, outwardly racist practice, they said it was to "teach a lesson about equity and systemic racism." In Buffalo, New York, teachers were instructed to tell students in middle and high school that "all whites play a part in perpetuating systemic racism." The curriculum was designed based on "Black Lives Matter principles." According to *City Journal*, the curriculum includes "'dismantling cisgender privilege,' creating 'queer-affirming network[s] where heteronormative thinking no longer exists,' and accelerating 'the disruption of Western nuclear family dynamics.'"[2]

In writing, that's a meaningless word salad. In practice, it's a hot, steaming plate of crazy, all served up by a bunch of whacko teachers. And at the head of all those teachers is a woman whom Mike Pompeo, the former secretary of state, has correctly dubbed "the most dangerous person in the world." Her name is Randi Weingarten, and as the head of the largest teachers' union in the country, she has allowed

2   Christopher F. Rufo, "Failure Factory," *City Journal*, February 23, 2021, https://www.city-journal.org/article/failure-factory (accessed September 3, 2024).

woke excesses to run *way* out of control. In a summer reading list provided to students by the American Federation of Teachers, Weingarten and her fellow administrators suggested *White Fragility* and *Gender Queer*, the latter of which contains graphic descriptions and images of oral sex as well as discussions on masturbation.

This kind of thing is happening all over the country. And in some cases, parents have no idea. In Buffalo, where only 18 percent of students are proficient in math by the fifth grade, teachers tell middle and high school students that the United States was designed for the "impoverishment of people of color and enrichment of white people," and that it "created a social system that had racist economic inequality built into its foundation." In high school, students are expected to "root out white supremacy" and "confront whiteness" in their classrooms.[3]

Also in Buffalo, students as young as five were shown a video of dead black children "speaking to them from beyond the grave about the dangers of being killed by 'racist police and state-sanctioned violence.'" When kids reach fifth grade, they're told that there is a "school-to-grave pipeline for black children and that, as adults, 'one million black people are locked in cages.'"[4]

I mean, *seriously?* When I was a kid, teachers tended to stick with *Reading Rainbow* or time-lapse videos about how plants got their food. Anyone showing cartoons about dead kids would, quite rightly, be put in a straitjacket and driven away in the back of a van.

Examples of this woke indoctrination could fill a book. And that book would probably need to be shelved in the horror section. If you think this is just a few isolated whack jobs in

3   Ibid.
4   Ibid.

California and Buffalo, think again. Over the past few years, as students have struggled to retain basic facts and pass their standardized tests, teachers all over the country have begun to embrace radical left-wing ideology in place of real teaching.

These people are failing our kids.

In February 2021 at the William D. Kelley School in Philadelphia, where literacy rates are among the lowest in the nation, kids in fifth grade were forced by their teachers to celebrate "black communism" while holding a pretend rally in honor of black radical activist Angela Davis, who had been credibly accused of three capital felonies and spent a year in jail before being acquitted by a jury in 1972. During the fake school rally in Philly, kids marched with signs expressing support for her, as well as other signs with slogans such as "Black Power," "Free Angela," and, for some reason, "Jail Trump."

At a middle school in Missouri around the same time, students were forced to locate themselves on an "oppression matrix" based on their skin color and to perform "land acknowledgments," during which they apologized for existing on land that was once owned by Native Americans. In Cupertino, California, students were forced to sit through a session in which a diversity consultant taught them how to "deconstruct their racial identities" before demanding that they write essays investigating their own "power and privilege." As an example, the instructor showed the kids an essay about "transgenderism and nonbinary sexuality."

You'll notice that over the past few pages, I've used the word "forced" when referring to the lessons being taught to children. That's because it's accurate. Unlike adults, kids don't have a choice about what happens to them when they go to school in the morning. They can't walk out and leave, and they can't object to what they're hearing. That's why it's important for parents to know what's going on in schools, and to have a say in designing the curricula. When they don't, ideologues take over, and children get insane lessons like the ones described here.

What troubles me about these "lessons" is not simply that they are factually inaccurate, although they are. It's not even that they waste valuable time that could be better spent teaching kids to read and do mathematics—something that is more important than ever given the well-documented decline in student performance that's occurred since the pandemic. My problem with these lessons is that they are downright *evil*. I just don't know how else to say it. As a Christian, all these teachings make me pretty sure that we are engaged in a battle in this nation the likes of which have dark roots. Getting on our knees to pray for our kids may be the only weapon that will save us.

On one side, we have those of us who remember school the way it was: a place where kids could go and learn how to be responsible citizens. There, they learned math, science, and a version of history that was untainted by radical left-wing ideology. *Way* back in the day, they learned useful skills, such as woodshop and home economics, but that ended when we decided that all kids, regardless of interest or aptitude, needed to be pushed toward expensive elite colleges. It's no accident that the period in which these kinds of lessons were the norm coincided with the greatest increase in prosperity for the middle class in the history of the United States. Since then, we've strayed far from our roots, taking prayer out of schools in 1963 and refusing to reintroduce Judeo-Christian values at every turn.

On the other side are those who seek to divide us based on race, gender, and religion. We have those who believe in the neo-Marxist idea that the world is divided into oppressors and oppressed, with nothing in between. According to these people, who have come to control many state boards of education, white children are oppressors because of their skin color, and black children are victims because of theirs. Parents who don't want their children to be told that they can magically change genders are oppressors, and the poor, confused kids are the oppressed. This idea comes straight from the work of Marxist philosophers such as Paulo Freire, whose book *Pedagogy of the Oppressed* is widely taught in elite graduate schools of education around the country.

At these schools, which include the Teachers College at Columbia University, and several state-run institutions, future teachers and administrators learn that it is their job to bring the "truth" to students, and often to do it behind the backs of parents. They learn that the nuclear family is outdated and oppressive, and that children should be taught primarily to enact revolutions rather than do simple mathematics. Rather than critical thinking, they teach "critical race theory" (CRT). According to a book introducing the concept to teachers in training, "In the mid-1990s, scholars in the field of education began drawing upon CRT as a framework to make sense of racism and inequality within educational systems. This was a landmark moment in the field. As was the case with the emergence of Marxist thought and postmodernist and post-structuralist feminist theory, the emergence of CRT radically transformed educational inquiry and discourse."[5]

Today, there is virtually no way to become a public-school teacher unless you've been certified by one of these woke grad schools of education. Teaching is one of the few professions that is extremely difficult to get into without a master's degree, and there is only one way to get a master's degree. Today, obtaining a teaching certification often entails submitting to insane ideas like "intersectionality," "equity," and "critical race

---

5 Isaac Gottesman, *The Critical Turn in Education: From Marxist Critique to Poststructuralist Feminism to Critical Theories of Race* (Milton Park, UK: Routledge, 2016), p. 11.

theory." The institutions that teach these ideas are powerful, in part because of how well-funded they are. As any good journalist knows, you always follow the money. According to the most recent data, more than *50 percent* of all state budgets go to K-12 education. That means we have allocated *half* our tax dollars to the wokest, least rigorous institutions in the country, and we've gotten nothing out of it other than bad ideas. We, the American taxpayers, are funding this indoctrination. We are paying for the demise of the next generation under these sick people.

Anyone who doubts that these bad ideas have fully taken hold need only scroll through the X feed of Chaya Raichik, owner of the social media account Libs of TikTok. There, you'll find plenty of examples of left-wing ideologues bragging about the ways they indoctrinate kids with woke nonsense. One, who was secretly recorded mid-rant by a student, says to a classroom of elementary school kids: "Turn off the Fox News! Do your parents listen to Fox News? Well, then most of y'all's parents are dumber than you, I'ma say that right now. My parents are friggin *dumb*! And the minute I figured that out, the world opened up!"[6] Now, I happen to work at Newsmax. Along with Fox, we are the top conservative TV news outlets in the country. We are reporting on this indoctrination while the legacy media is ignoring it. And they're ignoring it *because* they're part of the corporate woke agenda.

Another, who introduces herself as a "nonbinary teacher," speaks to a young girl while secretly recording it on her phone, chastising her for failing to call her "Teacher Robi" rather than "Mrs. Robi." A male teacher with a rainbow flag on his wall says that traditional teaching "concerns itself with positive

---

6   Campus Reform, "Compilation: Wildest Teacher Tik Tok Rants," November 5, 2021, https://www.youtube.com/watch?v=R5Z7bxNzn-w (accessed September 3, 2024).

behaviors, so we have to ask ourselves, okay what are those positive behaviors? And it's things like making sure that you're following directions, and making sure that you're sitting quietly, and making sure that you're in your seat. All these things that come from *white culture*. [That] is not a thing that's in many cultures. So, if we're positively enforcing these behaviors, we are by extension positively enforcing elements of white culture, which therefore keeps whiteness at the center, which is the definition of white supremacy."[7]

You might also look at the work of Project Veritas, which conducted several sting operations to reveal the true intentions of the organizations that supply schools with lesson plans in CRT and gender studies. In one, a consultant for public schools who doesn't know he's being recorded says that he's "an evil salesman," and that although Georgia, the state he lives in, has banned racist concepts such as CRT, he slips them in anyway.

"If you don't say the word 'critical race theory,'" he says, "you can teach it…. He's [Governor Brian Kemp] such an idiot…."[8]

Now, this raises a question. If CRT and all this neo-Marxist nonsense is so important to teach kids, why do school boards and teachers unions go to such great lengths to *hide* it? Why was the Libs of TikTok account repeatedly banned from pre-Musk Twitter for "violating the privacy" of teachers who *filmed themselves* posting unhinged rants and then posted them for all the world to see?

It doesn't take an investigative reporter to figure out the answer.

---

7   Ibid.

8   Project Veritas, "Breaking: @TeachingLabHQDirector @DrQuintinBostic Admits…" X, January 17, 2024, https://x.com/Project_Veritas/status/161 5484136197701632 (accessed September 3, 2024).

The new ideologues in our education system don't want parents to see what they're doing, because they don't see parents as allies. To them, we are the enemy. *We* are what stands between them and the impressionable brains of our children, which they are dying to fill with nonsensical concepts like *equity* and *white supremacy* and *interlocking matrices of transgender oppression.* The more we find out about what they're teaching our kids—that one's gender can be changed on a whim, for instance, or that women can have penises and men can give birth—the more outraged we get. And the more outraged we get, the more threatened they become. I'm sure they know that if we get outraged enough, they might have to go back to teaching basic reading and writing skills, which is a lot harder than putting on a fake protest while spouting a bunch of left-wing buzzwords.

So, they hide. They obfuscate. They coordinate with the mainstream media and the federal government to pretend that they are *not*, in fact, teaching CRT. Recently, they've told us that CRT doesn't even exist. Speaking on MSNBC during some of the most heated legislative debates on the issue, host Joy Reid called CRT "a myth" and "a delusion." Then, just a few nights later, she was talking to Nikole Hannah-Jones about what a tragedy it was that so many states are *banning* CRT.

In other words: Don't believe your lying eyes. Or your ears. Or the many examples of CRT in practice that opened this chapter (which, I'm sorry to say, barely scratch the surface).

This is plain evil.

And it's not new.

Throughout history, we've seen left-wing totalitarian regimes come for children, trying to drive a wedge between them and their parents. In fact, that's kind of their thing. In 1917, after the Russian Revolution, as the Heritage Foundation's Mike Gonzalez pointed out, a key figure in the Communist Party wrote, "The old family, narrow and petty, where the parents quarrel and are only interested in their own offspring, is not capable of educating the 'new person.'"[9] In post-revolutionary Soviet schools, students were often encouraged to spy on their parents, looking for signs that they weren't being sufficiently Marxist in the home, and report back to their teachers with the results.

Wherever radical left-wing ideology spread, parents and children were driven apart. In Hungary in 1919, the Communist Party established a state-run school to educate children about radical politics. The man behind it all was the education commissar, George Lukacs, who "instituted a system to instruct young children into sexual perversions."[10] His biographer, according to Mike Gonzalez, described the schools this way: "Special lectures were organized in schools and literature printed and distributed to 'instruct' children about free love, about the nature of sexual intercourse, about the archaic nature of bourgeois family codes, about the out-datedness of monogamy, and the irrelevance of religion, which deprives man of all pleasure. Children urged thus to reject and deride paternal authority and the authority of the church, and to ignore precepts of morality."[11]

In other words, young children were taught lessons about sex and the irrelevance of the nuclear family without their parents' knowledge.

Sound familiar?

How many situations have we seen lately in which young kids are being treated in a similar manner—being forced to endure story time from drag queens and transgender people with an obvious agenda to push?

---

9   Mike Gonzalez, "Socialism and Family," Heritage Foundation, March 1, 2022, https://www.heritage.org/marriage-and-family/commentary/socialism-and-family (accessed September 3, 2024).

10   Ibid.

11   Ibid.

Too many to count.

Throughout history, this trend has continued. After Fidel Castro and his guerilla soldiers took over Cuba in 1959, children were forced to inform on parents who didn't express enough support for the Revolution in the home. According to Che Guevara, Castro's murderous second in command, children were "malleable clay from which the new person could be built with none of the old defects."[12] In Germany, where the Hungarian education commissar fled after his state-run school collapsed after just over 130 days of existence, scholars such as Theodore Adorno and Herbert Marcuse—who, in later years, would become extremely influential to critical race theorists—wrote extensively about the need to destroy the nuclear family.

In China under the leadership of Chairman Mao Zedong, the world saw just how bad things could be when Marxist principles were put into practice. During the period known as the Cultural Revolution, people were forced to publicly recant all beliefs that didn't align with what the Communist Party believed. In state-run schools, children were taught that the ideals of their parents were outdated and dangerous. They were forced to inform on their family members to teachers and party officials.

It's no wonder that in Cupertino, California, in 2021, one of the parents whose child had been forced to endure a session on CRT and transgenderism was reminded of her family's experience during Mao's Cultural Revolution. Speaking to *City Journal* on the condition of anonymity, she said that these ideas divide society "between the oppressor and the oppressed, and since these identities are inborn characteristics people cannot change, the only way to change it is via

---

12   Che Guevara, "Socialism and Man in Cuba," March 12, 1965, https://www.marxists.org/archive/guevara/1965/03/man-socialism.htm (accessed September 3, 2024).

violent revolution…. Growing up in China, I had learned it many times. The outcome is the family will be ripped apart; husband hates wife, children hate parents. I think it is already happening here."[13]

Tragically, I think she's right.

Every day, the similarities between our current political moment and Mao's China come into sharper focus. Whenever someone is forced to apologize publicly for violating some new rule of the woke, it's impossible not to think of the "struggle sessions" that occurred all over China in the 1950s and '60s. During these public events, which were attended by people of all ages and income levels, people were forced to recant their "non-revolutionary" ideas. Those who refused were beaten. Often, children were forced to watch as their parents walked back public statements on the existence of God or the utility of capitalism, fearing that failure to do so might result in imprisonment or death. If citizens expressed doubt about the lies the government was telling them every day—about the size of crop harvests, for instance, or the basic principles of Marxism—they were immediately questioned by the authorities.

In part, the Communist Party was able to get away with this because it had effectively made a free and independent press illegal. The only media outlets people could access were the ones that the party controlled. Opposition was forbidden. Speaking out against the regime landed people in prison. The only option for citizens was to go along with the new, radical culture, which was imposed not only by the government but by other citizens. Everything they read in newspapers and heard on the radio confirmed that the regime was correct.

---

13 Christopher F. Rufo, "Woke Elementary," *City Journal*, January 13, 2021, https://www.city-journal.org/article/woke-elementary (accessed September 18, 2024).

In June 2024, I interviewed a woman named Lily Tang-Williams on *Newsline*. The previous month marked thirty-six years since Lily had left communist China as a teenager, escaping the absolute devastation of Mao's Cultural Revolution. At the time I interviewed her, Lily was running for Congress in New Hampshire. She had come a long way from the teenager who showed up in Austin, Texas, as an immigrant in the 1990s.

"The terms and tactics that the far Left and radical Democrats are using are very similar to what I saw in China," she told me. "And that includes weaponizing youth, turning young people against traditional families, and also to get people to fight against each other, to label people...and that includes the DEI and CRT.... I just want to sound the alarm. I recognize the similarities, and I wanted to run for Congress to...save people from that kind of Cultural Revolution."

Reading these comparisons, you might wonder if such a thing might be possible here in the United States. Could the government *really* exert that much control over the K-12 education system, shaming anyone who resisted into submission, sometimes through violent force? Wouldn't our rule of law prevent it from happening?

Ask Scott Smith.

In the beginning of 2021, Scott Smith was a plumber living happily in Loudoun County, Virginia. He ran a small business, sent his kids to public schools, and generally kept to himself.

One day, he got a call that his daughter had been sexually assaulted in a school bathroom. He drove to the school, where he was shocked to learn that the person who'd assaulted his daughter was a boy wearing girl's clothes. According to reporting by Luke Rosiak of *The Daily Wire*, Smith became irate, demanding that school officials call the police.

Which they did.

On *him*.

What followed was a series of events that are almost too shocking to believe. Rather than bringing the transgender student up on charges, the school protected him, not wanting to go against the woke ideologues on the faculty, or to make any unwanted headlines in the mainstream media (not that they would have reported on such a story anyway). That spring, officials simply transferred the boy to a different school, hoping to sweep the whole thing under the rug.

At the time, school board meetings had become hot beds of controversy. Parents who'd seen all the evil things their children were being taught during the COVID-19 lockdowns were finally allowed to show up and voice their concerns. I covered several of these events on *Newsline*, including once incident involving a series of math books that were found to contain cut-and-dry examples of CRT. Speaking over footage of the offending texts, which literally said that things such as "the right answer" did not exist, I could hardly believe what I was seeing.

Later in that same show, which aired in April 2022, I spoke with Brandon Michon, who was running for Congress at the time in Loudoun County, Virginia.

"What you really have is a big social agenda experiment going on," he told me. "We have the pushing down of ideologies and agendas into the most innocent and most easily influenced part of the population. What we need to focus on is reading, writing, science, history, arithmetic—the things we all grew up with—not telling my seven-year-old that she can change who she is sexually, not telling them that they're bad because of their skin color.... The last thing we should be telling people is that they should hate their neighbor, dislike someone because of their skin color, or dislike someone because of their religion.... We need to get back to teaching our children."

In Loudoun County, where Brandon Michon and Scott Smith's families lived, many parents were irate about new policies that would be enacted the following year. According to these policies, children would be free to use bathrooms and locker rooms that "best aligned with their gender identities." In other words, boys who said they were girls would now be free to go into the girls' locker room and get naked, no matter what the girls had to say about it.

As the parent of a young girl, I completely understood their anger.

But the members of the school board, nearly all of whom were Democrats, did *not* understand the anger. In fact, they mocked it. On June 22, during a particularly heated meeting, one member of the school board said, "To my knowledge, we do not have any record of assaults occurring in our restrooms." Later, referring to an article in *Time* magazine about transgender bathrooms, the same school board member said, "I think it's important to keep our perspective on this. We've heard several times tonight from our public speakers, but the predator transgender student or person simply does not exist."[14]

As he said this, Scott Smith sat quietly. He knew that assaults of young women were not, in fact, myths. It had happened to his own ninth-grade daughter. But members of the school board—who, it bears mentioning, had most likely been on board with the catchphrase "Believe All Women" during the #MeToo movement just a few months earlier—

---

14 Luke Rosiak, "Loudon County Schools Tried to Conceal Sexual Assault Against Daughter in Bathroom, Father Says," *The Daily Wire*, https://www.dailywire.com/news/loudoun-county-schools-tried-to-conceal-sexual-assault-against-daughter-in-bathroom-father-says (accessed September 18, 2024).

had refused to believe her. A scuffle began, it got loud, and Scott Smith made a noise. All around Smith, the parents went wild. Boos and jeers erupted from the crowd. According to *The Daily Wire*'s account of the story, a woman in a rainbow shirt told Smith that she "didn't believe" his daughter's story. He began to argue with her, using heated language and speaking at a high volume.

"Before he knew it," according to the piece, "he was hit in the face, handcuffed, and dragged across the floor with his pants pulled down."

That night, images of the incident led several mainstream news broadcasts. With almost no exceptions, the narrative was the same. The media painted Scott Smith as a deranged maniac. To them, he was the exact embodiment of the (imaginary) irate right-wing parents they'd been warning about for years—one who had the wrong ideas, and thus needed to be dealt with by force.

On *Buzzfeed News*, Smith's picture ran under the headline "A Man Was Arrested After a School Board Meeting Erupted in Protest Against Critical Race Theory." The accompanying video made it seem like it was Smith who caused the trouble. The sympathies of the reporter were clear, as always, from the story's first line: "One man was arrested and another detained for trespassing after a fight broke out during a raucous school board meeting in Virginia that was disrupted by parents protesting against critical race theory and a proposed policy for transgender students' rights." According to this frame, it was the crowd of concerned parents who were unreasonable, and the poor school board members were under attack. Similar stories ran on MSNBC and CNN in the days that followed.

It's worth noting, of course, that none of these outlets sent reporters down to Loudoun County to cover the story. They simply picked up the photograph from a wire service, guessed about the details, and printed their stories, which all adhered to the same ideological points.

And it was the wrong story.

Shortly after that narrative saturated the media landscape, the National Association of School Boards wrote a letter to the Biden administration claiming that "America's public schools and its education leaders [were] under an immediate threat."[15] They asked for assistance from federal law enforcement to deal with a "growing number of threats of violence and acts of intimidation occurring across the nation." As evidence, they cited twenty incidents that had occurred at school board meetings across the country (not a single one of which, as we would only find out later, involved any violence). One of them was the Scott Smith incident.

In this memo, the authors went as far as suggesting the PATRIOT Act be used to go after parents who speak out at school board meetings. Outrageous. This Bush-era law introduced after 9/11 is typically used to root out terrorists operating in the United States. So, the National Association of School Boards was, in effect, calling parents who advocated for their children potential domestic terrorists. The echoes of past left-wing totalitarian regimes could not be clearer. The scary thing is what happened next.

Less than a week later, Attorney General Merrick Garland responded by sending a memo to the FBI and other officials at the Department of Justice. Parroting the talking points he'd been given by the National Association of School Boards, he warned of a "disturbing spike in harassment, intimidation, and threats of violence against school administrators, board members, teachers, and staff who participate in the vital work

---

15   Press release, "Full NSBA Letter to Biden Administration and Department of Justice Memo," Parents Defending Education, November 29, 2021, https:// defendinged.org/press-releases/full-nsba-letter-to-biden-administration-and-department-of-justice-memo/ (accessed September 4, 2024).

of running our nation's public schools."[16] He instructed the FBI to look into the matter, once again treating parents like domestic terrorists.

All because some lazy journalists were willing to embrace the wrong story.

It took a young reporter for *The Daily Wire* named Luke Rosiak to get the *right* story. Over a period of a few weeks, Rosiak interviewed the main participants and dug into the public records involved. He learned that a police report had indeed been filed on the day of Smith's daughter's assault, and that the report included "two counts of forcible sodomy—one count of anal sodomy and one count of forcible fellatio." He learned that on the day Scott Smith went to the school to respond to the incident with his daughter, six police cars showed up to arrest him. Most shockingly of all, Rosiak learned that a few months after the school transferred the transgender student to a different school, he assaulted yet *another* young girl in a classroom.

These details weren't hard to find. Any reporter from a major outlet could have taken the same steps that Luke Rosiak did and written up the story. But no reporters did. They didn't do it because they knew that their bosses wouldn't condone it, and reporting anything negative about a trans child in school would cause an uproar among their liberal readership. They knew, like citizens in left-wing totalitarian countries have known for decades, that putting even one foot out of line when it comes to the radical ideology of the day can have disastrous consequences for one's reputation.

In the years since the incident at the school board meeting, Scott Smith has been issued a full pardon by Governor Glenn Youngkin of Virginia, who was elected largely because he took the side of the parents during his campaign for the

16   Ibid.

governorship. That pardon, I'm sure, owes a great deal to the excellent reporting that *The Daily Wire* published about the incident. And, in yet another twist, the prosecutor who zealously went after Scott Smith was wiped out at the ballot box the following November.

It's yet another reminder that getting the right story out to the public—scrutinizing the facts, stripping away all the ideology, and reporting the truth of what really happened—is vital to American democracy. Even after *The Daily Wire*'s bombshell reporting on the subject, none of the "big three" networks covered the Loudoun County story. Without journalists who are willing to do their jobs, society falls to partisan ideologues who only want to push a radical agenda.

Sadly, that's still happening.

In January 2024, a reporter at the *New York Times* published a surprisingly thorough, ideology-free article titled "When Children Say They're Trans." In the piece, the reporter pointed out that according to current practices at most schools, teachers are not required to tell parents when children express a wish to medically transition to a different gender.

Instead, according to the article, kids are allowed to change their names, use different bathrooms, and refer to themselves using any pronouns they wish, all without their teachers ever speaking to their parents. One mother, whose child began transitioning from a girl to a boy at school, only noticed the change when she saw a different name at the top of one of her daughter's assignments.

As soon as the article was published, there was outcry from the social justice Left. The organization GLAAD parked a truck outside the newspaper's headquarters. On it, written in red ink, were the words "THE SCIENCE IS SETTLED."

The previous year, GLAAD had issued a statement about the newspaper's coverage of trans issues, which had begun to stray ever so slightly from the Democratic Party line. "A year's worth of stories from the *Times* Science Desk have undermined support for transgender youth," the group wrote, "by purporting dangerous opinions from non-experts as objective facts, neglecting both medical science and the overwhelming consensus support for trans healthcare among major medical associations, while equating medical expertise to anti-LGBTQ lawmaker opinion."

Please.

"The science," as anyone who's done more than ten seconds of research into this topic knows, is far from settled.

According to a new, non-partisan review conducted in Britain, the evidence for "gender-affirming care" in children is virtually nonexistent. The author, Hillary Cass, found that while "a considerable amount of research had been published in [the field of youth gender medicine], systematic evidence reviews demonstrated the poor quality of the published studies, meaning there is not a reliable evidence base upon which to make clinical decisions."[17]

But the woke activists in the United States, particularly those who work with children, have not been swayed by the evidence. Neither has the Biden administration, which says that "gender-affirming care" for minors is "crucial to [their] overall health and well-being." They love it *so* much, in fact, that they even declared a Transgender Day of Visibility on the same day as Easter Sunday in 2024, dealing a double slap in the face to Christians. According to Rachel Levine, a transgender person who led the Department of Health and Human

---

17 "The Cass Review: Independent Review of Gender Identity Services for Children and Young People," April 2024, https://cass.independent-review. uk/home/publications/final-report/ (accessed September 4, 2024).

Services under Joe Biden—it is possible for young people to go through "the wrong puberty."

In journalism, one of the cardinal rules is to ignore jargon and euphemistic language. When politicians try to feed you a line about "collateral damage" or "irregularities," you're supposed to find out what those phrases are *really* referring to. In the case of "gender-affirming care," what we're talking about is the physical mutilation and forced sterilization of children. For boys, it means prescribing off-label drugs to stop the onset of puberty and then slicing up the penis to turn it into something resembling a vagina; for girls, it means prescribing similar drugs, then conducting a double mastectomy and performing genital surgery. The next time the Biden administration puts out a proclamation about the importance of "gender-affirming care" for young people, *that* is what you should think about. Because that is what the words really mean.

Recently, we've learned that the puberty-blocking drugs that are often prescribed to children can have devastating health effects. Even ABC News has been forced to report on the Food and Drug Administration's finding that one of the main puberty blocking drugs has been found to have links to "Pseudotumor cerebri, also known as idiopathic intracranial hypertension, [which] occurs when the pressure inside your skull spontaneously increases, which can cause brain swelling, severe headaches, nausea, double vision, and even permanent vision loss, according to the Mayo Clinic."[18]

One need only read Abigail Shrier's excellent book *Irreversible Damage* to find out just how horrible these procedures can be for young children, many of whom come to

---

18   Alec Schemmel, "FDA warns puberty blocker may cause brain swelling, vision loss in children," ABC News 4, July 26, 2022, updated August 5, 2022, https://abcnews4.com/news/nation-world/fda-warns-puberty-blocker-may-cause-brain-swelling-vision-loss-in-children-rachel-levine (accessed September 4, 2024).

regret their decision to transition later in life. In the book, she tells stories of young girls who are filled with regret because their procedures have left them unable to have babies. No matter how many surgeries they have to correct the procedures, which gender doctors often claim are completely reversible, they'll never be able to experience the miracle of childbirth. No one has done a better job than Abigail Shrier of sifting through the vague language surrounding gender theory and exposing the truth behind it.

In an op-ed in her local newspaper *The Albuquerque Journal*, a woman named Trisha Mosley wrote about the heartbreaking journey she took, all aided by evil doctors.

"I was a minor who identified as transgender," she writes, "and irreversibly changed my body through drugs and surgery under the misconception that it was possible to change sex and that this would cure my real mental struggles. Back then, I was confident that I knew what I was doing and wanted this 'treatment.' I thought I would never want children or change my mind about wanting to appear like a man."[19]

No one knows this better than my pal Oli London, the author of *Gender Madness* and a frequent guest on *Newsline*. Speaking about the Cass Report, Oli said, "The vast majority of transgender children completely grow out of their gender dysphoria into adulthood. [A study in the Netherlands] found that 96 percent of them don't want to be trans after a certain age. It's a very harmful trend, and parents should not be pushing this on their kids."

Oli knows what he's talking about. As a young person, he suffered from gender dysphoria and underwent several

---

19 Prisha Mosley, "OPINION: 'Gender ideology' robbed me of my childhood and future health," *The Albuquerque Journal*, June 17, 2024, https://www.abqjournal.com/opinion/opinion-gender-ideology-robbed-me-of-my-childhood-and-future-health/article_b5379eda-29f7-11ef-9944-cfd1586e5afb.html (accessed September 18, 2024).

surgeries that were supposed to make him look like a Korean woman. It wasn't until years later that he realized the error of his ways and came to terms with what he'd done to his body; today, he speaks out against gender madness and tries to warn young people not to go down the same harmful path that he did.

Unfortunately, today's popular media organizations don't seem interested in exposing the truth about these new bizarre medical procedures. Instead, they take their cues from the party in charge and try not to upset left-wing activists. As the writer Jesse Singal has recently pointed out, these outlets use nearly identical language to assure the public that nothing is wrong with "gender-affirming care" for minors. In some cases, the sentences are literally the same. In a story about the recent developments surrounding youth gender medicine in the United Kingdom, a writer for CNN reported accurately that doctors in the UK will no longer be giving puberty blockers to minors. But that CNN reporter also included a strange sentence in her article: "Gender-affirming care is medically necessary, evidence-based care that uses a multidisciplinary approach to help a person transition from their assigned gender—the one the person was designated at birth—to their affirmed gender—the gender by which one wants to be known."

"There's a strong case to be made," Singal writes, "that CNN's sentence, as written, is false. Gender medicine is at best unproven, when it comes to the standards society (and regulatory bodies) expects medical researchers to adhere to. The situation with youth gender medicine is particularly dicey, given that this is a newer area of medicine suffering from an even severer paucity of quality studies."[20]

---

20   Jesse Singal, "Why Is The Same Misleading Language About Youth Gender Medicine Copied And Pasted Into Dozens Of CNN.com Articles?" Singal-Minded, March 22, 2024, https://jessesingal.substack.com/p/why-is-the-same-misleading-language (accessed September 18, 2024).

Where are the fact-checkers?

Even worse perhaps, he goes on to note that this sentence, or close variants of it, has been copied and pasted into more than *thirty* CNN stories over the past two years alone. At most reputable news organizations, that would expose every reporter involved to charges of lazy reporting. But at CNN, as well as many of the other mainstream media organizations, lazy reporting is often part of the job description.

Obviously, CNN knows what happens when publications report accurately about the left-wing fad of the moment. They get trucks parked outside their headquarters with insane claims about youth gender medicine. Every day, publications that dare to tell the truth about youth gender medicine are similarly harassed and threatened online. So, they copy and paste the propaganda, trying to avoid getting called out by the regime. They are doing, in other words, exactly the *opposite* of what good journalists are supposed to do.

All over the country, people who speak out against the prevailing left-wing orthodoxy are smeared as fascists and intolerant menaces. That's especially true for parents who demand to have a say in the education of their children—or even the parents of children who've been misled by teachers into believing they can magically change their gender at will. If you doubt this, consider the uproar that has occurred in recent years over what material should and should not be allowed in school libraries.

On one side, we have people who believe that children should be reading age-appropriate material—or, at the very least, material that does not contain graphic depictions of adult sexual acts or language about sex changes. On the other side, we have people who believe that children should be seeing *more* of this stuff, and that anyone who says otherwise is an intolerant bigot who wants to "ban books."

Consider what happened when Governor Ron DeSantis of Florida attempted to pass a bill that would, in the language of the law, prohibit "classroom instruction…on sexual orientation or gender identity" in "kindergarten through grade 3 or in a manner that is not age-appropriate or developmentally appropriate." In a matter of days, progressive activists had smeared the law as Florida's "Don't Say Gay" bill, pretending that it didn't allow children even to utter the word "gay" in classrooms. They even put up a billboard on I-95 in South Florida that read "SAY GAY."

Around the time the bill was being debated, Floridian Dave Rubin—who happens to *be* gay and a father—joined me on my show to call out the B.S. He said, "I fled California because of this nonsense, came here to Florida, and now it's happening here! I'm going to have to do the underground bunker thing. That's where this is going to end up.… This is what the media and the Democrats do with absolutely everything.… They blow up nothingness into some kind of hateful, homophobic, transphobic, racist, blah blah blah."

The same goes with so-called book banning.

Every day, we see editorials accusing conservative parents of being somehow on par with the Nazis. A September 2023 piece in *The New Republic* was titled "Everything You Need to Know about the Right-Wing War on Books." *The Guardian* declared, "Republicans will do anything to ban books."

Again, this is the wrong story. For decades, parents have had the right to decide which books are suitable for children in public schools. That's part of their duty as parents. No conservatives, as far as I can tell, are demanding that books no longer be allowed to be printed or sold in the United States. They are simply having debates about which books their children should be reading in school—which, as parents, is exactly what they're supposed to do.

Liberals, on the other hand, seem to *love* banning books.

You might remember the last chapter, when I mentioned the woke employees at publishing houses who routinely stage walkouts to protest books that hurt their feelings. *That* is book banning, or at least *attempted* book banning. Every few months there is another story about left-wing psychos trying to shut down ideas they don't like. Often, these ideas come in the form of books—which, no matter what the diversity czars in our public schools tell you, are not "tools of white supremacy."

Consider that when Abigail Shrier's *Irreversible Damage* came out, trans activists worked their butts off to get it pulled from store shelves. A lawyer at the American Civil Liberties Union—who, ironically, is the representative of a free speech organization—called the book "a dangerous polemic with a goal of making people not trans." Near the end of her message, she said, "Stopping the circulation of this book and these ideas is 100 percent a hill I will die on."[21] Under pressure from these activists, several stores, including Target, pulled the book. Similar campaigns have been waged to stop the sale of books by J.K. Rowling, who has shown similar resilience in the face of threats from the transgender activist community.

Again, reporting the facts accurately is vital here. Pushing back against propaganda is more important than it's ever been. Thankfully, some people are still willing to tell kids the right story about the United States of America. A few years ago, writers Bethany Mandel and Karol Markowicz, author of the book *Stolen Youth*, collaborated to begin a series of children's books called *Heroes of Liberty*, which tell the stories of famous Americans who believe in all the values the Left is currently

---

21 Charlotte Hays, "Some in ACLU Have New Cause: Book Banning," Independent Women's Forum, November 26, 2020, https://www.iwf.org/2020/11/16/some-in-aclu-have-new-cause-book-banning/ (accessed September 4, 2024).

attacking.[22] Some parents have decided that homeschooling is the right way to go. I don't blame them. Given what awaits our kids in classrooms these days, it's tempting to keep them at home for as long as possible.

Unfortunately, the indoctrination doesn't end once kids cross the high school graduation stage and head off to college.

That's when it really begins.

---

22 Heroes of Liberty, "American Values One Story at a Time," https://heroesof-liberty.com (accessed September 4, 2024).

CHAPTER FOUR

UNIVERSITIES: THE LONG GAME

On Saturday, October 7, 2023, I was up early, preparing to cover a Trump rally that evening in Waterloo, Iowa. I reached for my phone, checked my inbox, and found a devastating update. Just a few minutes earlier, Israel had been attacked by members of the Islamic terror group Hamas. Children had been brutally murdered. Women had been taken hostage. The footage of these terrorists invading unsuspecting neighborhoods, and even parachuting into a music festival, were horrifying.

As I scrolled through the footage online, I knew that this day would be seared into history. I knew that my news coverage that night would be focused on the details of this purely evil attack. Already, the word "holocaust" was in the air. By the time I arrived at the studio, the sequence of events had become clear.

Terrorists had broken the barrier between Gaza and Israel, killing hundreds of people as they laughed and screamed *Allahu Akbar*. In grainy, low-resolution videos, I saw the corpses of young women being dragged through the street by terrorists grinning ear to ear. I saw people being shot in the streets with machine guns, crying helplessly before they were killed. It didn't take long to figure out that Hamas, a group whose main goal (according to its own charter) is to kill every Jew on the face of the earth, was responsible.[1]

Later that night, as I was on the air, former president Trump addressed the horrific events directly from his rally stage, saying that it was Joe Biden's weakness on the world stage that made Hamas feel emboldened to attack.

Over the next few days, the death counts mounted, and the grisly details were revealed. We learned that Hamas had filmed the attacks purposely, wanting to send a message to the world. One of these videos showed a young man on the phone with his parents, bragging ecstatically about what he'd done.

"I've killed ten Jews! Look how many I killed with my own hands," he says. "Your son killed Jews! Mom, your son is a hero!"

Other footage showed women being decapitated and loaded into pickup trucks, where live hostages were forced to sit beside the bodies. Stories from survivors of the massacre—which Hamas called *Al Aqsa*, or "the flood" in Arabic—told harrowing stories about trying to hide from the terrorists. One boy whose father had been killed recounts seeing one of the Hamas murderers going through his refrigerator.

"Stop," he said. "That's my mother's food."

To which the terrorist replied: "Where's your mother? I want her, too."

In the end, more than 1,500 people were murdered. The attack was the greatest loss of Jewish life in a single day since the Holocaust. It was also a stark reminder that in many parts of the world, especially those ruled by militant Islam, antisemitism is still shockingly widespread. In some countries, it's part of daily life. According to polls conducted by the Pew

---

1   Bruce Hoffman, "Understanding Hamas's Genocidal Ideology," *The Atlantic*, October 10, 2023, https://www.theatlantic.com/international/archive/2023/10/hamas-covenant-israel-attack-war-genocide/675602/ (accessed September 4, 2024).

Research Center in 2009, more than 90 percent of people polled in Muslim nations had "overwhelmingly unfavorable" views about the Jewish people.[2]

Following the attack, I spoke with Caroline Glick, who joined the coverage that night and soon became a regular commentator on my show. She said, "I think what we're seeing here is a combination of absolute prejudice against Jews, where Jewish women simply don't matter."

In many ways, this seemed like the moment that sick, left-wing social justice warriors on American college campuses had been waiting for. After all, they had talked about almost nothing for the past few years *other* than how much they hated Nazis. In the aftermath of the Unite the Right rally in Charlottesville, when a bunch of idiots with tiki torches marched through town yelling "Jews will not replace us," counter-protests were held on campuses all over the country. A student group at Harvard declared, "hate will not be tolerated." Columbia University Democrats said, "we stand with the Jewish people."

In the years that followed, college kids began hurling the words "Nazi" and "fascist" around like frisbees. Anyone they disagreed with was a fascist. When a speaker came to campus bearing a message that conflicted with the woke, neo-Marxist dogma that these kids had all been spoon-fed since birth, they'd shout them down and call them a Nazi.

Your new roommate says she's pro-life?

Call her a Nazi.

A student group invites a Republican to give a guest lecture?

Call them all Nazis.

The campus coffee shop says they're out of vegan milk?

---

2   Amir Mizroch, "Poll: 90% of ME views Jews Unfavorably," *The Jerusalem Post*, February 9, 2010, https://www.jpost.com/middle-east/poll-90-percent-of-me-views-jews-unfavorably (accessed September 4, 2024).

Call them Nazis, run out of the building, and go report a hate crime.

In the fall of 2017, students at William & Mary University shut down a speech by a lawyer for the American Civil Liberties Union, calling her a Nazi because the ACLU had defended some marchers at Charlottesville. A few weeks later, students at the University of Oregon interrupted a speech by the college president, calling him a Nazi and a fascist. One week after *that*, protestors at UCLA interrupted a talk titled "What Is Civil Discourse? Challenging Hate Speech in a Free Society," calling everyone on the stage Nazis. (It didn't seem to matter that the talk was sponsored by the United States Holocaust Memorial Museum.)

In that year alone, dozens of speeches were shut down because students believed the speakers were fascists. The conservative Jewish commentator Ben Shapiro had to hire private security when students attempted to beat him with bricks on the campus of UCLA, chanting that he was a Nazi. Heather Mac Donald, a columnist for the *Wall Street Journal* and a fellow at the Manhattan Institute, was physically attacked on the campus of Claremont-McKenna College because students believed she was a Nazi. President Trump—whose daughter and son-in-law are both Jewish—was called a Nazi by left-wing mobs in almost every city he traveled to.

So, you might think that in the aftermath of the worst attack on the Jewish people since the dissolution of the *actual* Nazi party, these kids would head straight to the quad and protest.

Which they did.

Just not for the side most people were expecting.

Beginning almost immediately after the attacks of October 7, before Israel had fired a single rocket in retaliation, small demonstrations were held on campuses all over the country— *in support of Hamas*. Immediately, a group called Students for

Justice in Palestine released the following statement, which appears to have been written before the bloodshed had even stopped: "National liberation is near—glory to our resistance, to our martyrs, and to our steadfast people!... Resistance comes in all forms—armed struggle, general strikes, and popular demonstrations. All of it is legitimate, and all of it is necessary."

At Columbia University, which sits on the Upper West Side of Manhattan, students gathered on the quad with signs reading "From the river to the sea, Palestine will be free." This chant, which is an explicit call for the elimination of the state of Israel, could soon be heard on college campuses all over the country. At Stanford University, a Jewish woman was surrounded by a left-wing mob, which called her "a dirty Jew, a child killer, and a colonizer," among other things. At Yale University, a student stood in the middle of the quad with a sign reading "Al-Qassam's Next Targets." (The Al-Qassam Brigades are the military wing of Hamas.) The arrow on the sign pointed directly at a group of Jewish students across the quad.

At Cornell University, a *professor* got onstage one week after the attacks of October 7 and described how he felt watching them occur. "We were able to breathe," he said. "They were able to breathe for the first time in years. It was exhilarating. It was energizing. And if they weren't exhilarated by this challenge to the monopoly of violence, by this shifting of the balance of power, then they would not be human. I was exhilarated."[3]

At the White House, future presidential candidate Kamala Harris celebrated with a barbecue the next day. And when the

3   Sofia Rubinson, "Cornell Professor 'Exhilarated' by Hamas's Attack Defends Remark," *The Cornell Daily Sun*, October 16, 2023, https://cornellsun. com/2023/10/16/cornell-professor-exhilarated-by-hamass-attack-de- fends-remark/#:~:text="Who%20were%20able%20to%20breathe,they%20 would%20not%20be%20human (accessed September 4, 2024).

White House finally *did* get around to putting out a statement, it condemned antisemitism *and* Islamophobia in the same sentence!

Do you *really* want people like this teaching your kids or leading our country?

So, to recap: According to today's college students, a professor who wants to present data on police violence is a Nazi, and so is everyone who's ever voted for Donald Trump. But religious fanatics who break through fences and murder Jews—and who repeatedly say that they want every last Jew wiped from the face of the earth—are "martyrs" and brave heroes of the "resistance."

Confused?

You're not alone.

As these demonstrations unfolded, most people across the country were surprised and horrified. Although they had heard scattered anecdotes about chaos on college campuses, they never thought it would lead to widespread support for a terror group like Hamas. The shock intensified in December 2023, when the presidents of Harvard University, MIT, and the University of Pennsylvania testified before Congress about the increasing wave of antisemitism on campus.

When Congresswoman Elise Stefanik asked Claudine Gay, the president of Harvard, whether calling for the murder of Jews would violate university policy, Gay said that it might, but only if the threats were "actionable." Later on in her testimony, Gay—who would later be fired after it was revealed that much of the material in her published work had been plagiarized—could not give a simple answer to the question of whether calling for the elimination of the Jewish people from the face of the earth violated the policies of Harvard University. By the end of the summer of 2024, every university president who testified at that hearing—as well as the president of Columbia University—would step down due to their mishandling of pro-Hamas protests on campus.

How could it be, you might wonder, that the Jewish people, who have suffered more than any group in the history of the world, are offered no protection by our nation's major universities?

Well, for one thing, they're white.

According to the left-wing, neo-Marxist doctrine that has come to dominate our university system, the world is divided into oppressed people and their oppressors. The oppressed people, according to this deranged theory, are almost always "people of color." Oppressors, on the other hand, are almost always white. It doesn't matter if the "people of color" are terrorists carrying machine guns and machetes, chanting for the blood of the Jews. They are, in the eyes of left-wing intellectuals, still the victims.

As the writer Douglas Murray pointed out in his book *The Madness of Crowds*, this hierarchy almost exactly mirrors the "pyramid of oppression" that used to appear in Communist newspapers in the early twentieth century. Only now, instead of evil capitalists at the top and the working classes at the bottom, the whole thing has expanded and gotten much more complex.

"At the top of the hierarchy," he writes, "are people who are white, male, and heterosexual. They do not need to be rich, but matters are made worse if they are. Beneath these tyrannical male overlords are all the minorities: most noticeably the gays, anyone who isn't white, people who are women and also people who are trans. These individuals are kept down, oppressed, sidelined, and otherwise made insignificant by the white, patriarchal, heterosexual, 'cis' system. Just as Marxism was meant to free the laborer and share the wealth around, so in this new version of an old claim, the power of the patriarchal white males must be taken away and shared around more fairly and with the relevant minority groups."[4]

In the aftermath of the antisemitism hearings, things didn't quiet down on campus. They only got more insane. All over the country, tents went up on quads, and students refused to leave until Israel stopped hunting down Hamas. At Yale University, a Palestinian group surrounded Jewish students as they walked between buildings, calling them "Zionists" and screaming that they were not welcome on campus. At Columbia, Jews were told to "go back to Poland" while massive crowds screamed, "Say it loud and clear, we don't want no Zionists here."[5] Across the street at Barnard College, the women's institution that somehow manages to be twice as insanely liberal as its sister school, Columbia, the daughter of Representative Ilhan Omar was arrested for protesting on campus.

The same activists who once balked at the phrase "Jews will not replace us" were now saying exactly the same thing. Screaming it, in fact. The same people who once chanted "Believe all women" in the streets were claiming that Israeli women had never been raped by Hamas terrorists, despite documentary evidence to the contrary. Again, the radical Left seems to add a new caveat to that slogan, "Believe all women," every day. If you're a woman who's been sexually assaulted, you should report it—just not if you're an Israeli woman who's been raped by a terrorist, or an innocent high school girl who's been raped in the girl's bathroom by a boy in a dress. In those cases, the male who raped you is, somehow, the victim, and you're just the white oppressor. On my show, *Newsline*, the

---

4   Douglas Murray, *The Madness of Crowds: Gender Race, and Identity* (London: Bloomsbury Continuum, 2019), p. 52.

5   Bari Weiss, "They Were Assaulted on Campus for Being Jews," The Free Press, April 21, 2024, https://www.thefp.com/p/they-were-assaulted-on-campus-for (accessed September 4, 2024).

writer Benjamin Weingarten of *The Federalist* described it as "#MeToo unless you're a Jew."

He was so right!

Throughout the spring of 2024, new left-wing groups appeared to protest Israel. Each one was stupider than the last. "Queers for Palestine" marched beside banners reading "Palestine: A Reproductive Justice Issue." Of course, such signs would not be tolerated in Gaza, where Hamas rules with an iron fist. There, anyone who describes themselves as "queer" would (literally) be thrown off a tall building immediately. Yet the same people who call American Christians "fascists" for opposing abortion will gladly look the other way when religious fanatics overseas murder people for being gay, as long as those religious fanatics are Muslim "people of color." If you need proof of this, just look at how Congresswoman Pramila Jayapal flies the Pride flag right beside the Palestinian flag outside her office.

That April at Columbia, students smashed the windows and broke down the doors of Hamilton Hall on campus, occupying the building and refusing to allow classes to be held. During a press conference, a graduate student who was at the university learning to "see everything through a Marxist lens," according to the university's website, demanded food and water for her and her fellow protestors…just a few *hours* after they'd broken in. (Of course, the Soros-funded district attorney Alvin Bragg would later drop all charges—likely because he was busy trying to prosecute a certain former president.)

"Like, could people please have a glass of water?" she asked. "Do you want students to die of dehydration or starvation or get severely ill even if they disagree with you? If the answer is no, then you should allow basic, I mean, it's crazy to say because we're on an Ivy League campus, but this is like basic humanitarian aid we're asking for."

After a brief exchange with a journalist in the crowd, she said, "We're just asking [the university] not to violently stop us from bringing in basic humanitarian aid."

The journalist—who's obviously been well trained in dealing with crazy people—asked if the university *had*, in fact, tried to violently stop anyone from bringing food and water into the building.

The student paused, looked around, and said, "…I don't know."

Aside from being a great example of what can happen when journalists ask the right questions, this incident reveals something about modern college students. They want to be victims more than anything. They want it so bad that they'll pretend to be oppressed in the middle of one of the wealthiest zip codes in the country, studying at what used to be one of this country's most prestigious universities, for the status that being oppressed gets them. In their minds, these students are continuing the struggle of the civil rights movement that began in the 1960s. And it doesn't seem odd to them that they're doing so by screaming in the faces of anyone who looks Jewish.

As these protests went on, many people expressed outrage at just how wicked and blatantly antisemitic these woke kids were getting. On April 24, I interviewed two Jewish students named Alon and Katie, both of whom asked to be identified by their first names only. Speaking about the school's recent decision to cancel graduation ceremonies and take classes online, Alon said, "I can tell you that there are friends of mine who are graduate students who have been requesting reimbursement for meal plans that they can't use, for library resources that they can't use, and they were told by admin that this is a no-go. None of the money is coming back. So, we're not getting anything that we're paying for.… We are being prevented from using resources that everyone else has."

When I asked Katie what message she wanted to leave my viewers with, she said, "My only thought is that these people are clearly missing the American values system, and all kinds of religious values as well. This is a morality issue. This goes way beyond this specific issue.... If this was happening to any other minority group, this would not be tolerated. And the fact that this is tolerated, the fact that they're allowed to say 'death to Jews,' and that we're allowed to be discriminated against just for existing on campus is a slap in the face to anyone that has the American dream like I did, who worked hard to get to Columbia."

On April 25, I interviewed Representative Anthony D'Esposito of New York, who had recently spoken up for Jewish students on Columbia's campus. Describing hecklers who were attempting to combat his positive message, he said, "It was disappointing. Yesterday, we were there to speak to everyone—the people who disagreed with us, and the people who agreed with us. There were students from both sides of this equation that wanted to hear what their elected officials had to say. But because of the loud, the obnoxious, those spewing hate, some of them weren't able to. It was a perfect example of what is happening on our college campuses throughout this country. And my statement to them yesterday was very clear. Just that morning, the protestors at Columbia were endorsed by Hamas. Hamas is a terrorist organization that brutally attacked, brutally murdered, and brutally raped individuals on October 7. If that doesn't tell you what our issue is here, I'm not sure what will."

Robert Kraft, owner of the New England Patriots and a Columbia grad, expressed similar dismay at the rank hatred that was flowing from his alma mater. In an op-ed for the *New York Post*, he wrote, "The Columbia I loved is no longer a place I know.... Those defining principles, once so revered, have been sacrificed by professors keen to use the classroom and the campus as a bully pulpit to promote their personal political viewpoints as opposed to fostering critical thinking—they preach eliminationist rhetoric championed by unchecked and dangerous activist groups."[6] It's no wonder that Kraft, ever the great businessman, pulled his funding from the university.

In the months that followed these protests, many people have attempted to uncover exactly how a bunch of college kids (often funded by the Democrats' biggest dark money donors) came to embrace such horrible ideas. Some have suggested that the kids might just be bored and gullible, willing to chant along with anything that rhymes. There's some truth to this. In the immediate aftermath of the attacks of October 7, a journalist waded into the crowd at a protest to ask which "river" and which "sea" the kids had meant when they chanted "from the river to the sea." They confessed that they didn't know.

A few weeks later, students at Columbia University were heard calling for "infantada," a mispronunciation of the Arabic word *intifada*, meaning the "uprising" against the Jews.

However, I believe this situation is much more sinister than a bunch of misinformed kids chanting slogans. At the very least, that's not the whole story. And in journalism, having only half the story is as good as having the *wrong* story. The decay of our college campuses is not an accident. In fact, it's part of a much greater plot to destabilize the United States of America—one that has been going on for some time.

If you need proof, take a look at who's funding it. According to a recent report in *Politico*, some of the largest funders of anti-Israel protests have also donated to the campaign of Joe Biden; they are, according to the article, "some

---

6   Robert Kraft, "Campus leaders must show courage and stop radical professors from poisoning young minds," *New York Post*, April 24, 2024, https://nypost.com/2024/04/24/opinion/campus-leaders-must-show-courage-and-stop-radical-profs-from-poisoning-young-minds/ (accessed September 4, 2024).

of the biggest names in Democratic circles: Soros, Rockefeller and Pritzker."[7]

The article goes on to say, "Two of the organizers supporting the protests at Columbia University and on other campuses are Jewish Voice for Peace and IfNotNow. Both are supported by the Tides Foundation, which is seeded by Democratic megadonor George Soros and was previously supported by the Bill and Melinda Gates Foundation."

This is calculated. It's well-funded. And it's decades old.

The neo-Marxist radicals who are currently destroying this country—toppling our statues, poisoning the minds of our children, and attempting to redefine society from the inside out—didn't just appear. For years, they've been sitting in their offices at colleges all over the country, working on crackpot theories, waiting for the right moment to carry out their plans, knowing the perfect firestorm would eventually appear and it did. Finally, they were gifted a generation of kids coddled and mis-educated enough to put those ideas into action, and we began to see the violent chaos that's unfolding today.

These people have been playing the long game.

And now, after decades of work, with the country teetering on the brink of all-out collapse, it's finally paying off.

In the late 1980s, when I was a high school student just beginning to pay attention to the evening news, I noticed that one story seemed to play out again and again. Somewhere overseas, in Europe or farther east, a communist government I'd never heard of would topple. There would be massive unrest, people

7   Shia Kapos, "Pro-Palestinian protestors are backed by a surprising source: Biden's biggest donors," *Politico*, May 5, 2024, https://www.politico.com/news/2024/05/05/pro-palestinian-protests-columbia-university-funding-donors-00156135 (accessed September 5, 2024).

would march in the streets, and then the country would simply fall apart.

It happened in Poland in 1989. A few months later, the Berlin Wall fell, bringing East Germany and West Germany together. When the Soviet Union fell apart in 1991, it seemed that the Cold War was finally over. Even to a kid who didn't know much about world politics, the score seemed clear.

America: 1.

Marxists: 0.

It was no wonder. Throughout the twentieth century, Marxism had brought nothing but misery to millions of people. Peasants in Ukraine had starved when Joseph Stalin collectivized farming in the Soviet Union. The same thing had happened to the Chinese during Mao Zedong's Great Leap Forward. And those who didn't starve were often jailed, beaten, or killed for disagreeing with the totalitarian governments that attempted to implement Karl Marx's policies—which, as anyone who's ever taken a basic economics course can figure out, just don't work.

For Marxist professors in the United States, this should have been the final nail in the coffin, a sign that it was time to put down the books, go outside, and get real jobs. I know that if *I* had come up theories that resulted in hundreds of millions of deaths, I probably would have tried a different line of work. Fashion design, maybe. Or baking. Something that didn't involve restructuring society from the ground up.

But that's not what the Marxists did.

Instead, they doubled down on their deranged ideology, trying to make it more palatable to American universities.

And it worked.

In October 1989, the *New York Times* ran an article titled "The Mainstreaming of Marxism at U.S. Colleges." In it, a reporter named Felicity Barringer writes, "As Karl Marx's ideological heirs in Communist nations struggle to transform his political legacy, his intellectual heirs on American campuses have virtually completed their own transformation from brash, beleaguered outsiders to assimilated academic insiders."[8]

At colleges all over the United States, left-wing professors who believed that capitalism was exploitative and that it needed to be overthrown by violent revolution moved into positions of power. They were granted tenure, and they began indoctrinating a new generation of kids. It's no accident that this "mainstreaming of Marxism" at US colleges coincides perfectly with the sudden rise of "political correctness" that happened in the early 1990s.

This was all part of the plan.

Decades earlier, in the late 1960s, it was becoming clear to left-wing groups that violent revolution was probably not going to work out—especially not in the United States, where people tended to be pretty happy about their lives under freedom and capitalism. (*Weird*, huh?) Every time they'd tried to implement Marx's dream of a violent revolution, they'd ended up on the wrong side of public opinion. It had happened in Germany, where left-wing groups routinely rioted in the streets. In 1968, it happened on a flight to Israel, when left-wing terrorists from the Palestinian Black September movement hijacked a plane, separating Jews from non-Jews in an early attempt to "free Palestine."

Watching all this unfold, a student activist in West Germany named Rudi Dutschke came up with a new plan of attack. Rather than throwing bombs and mobbing buildings, left-wing groups would shape up a little—or at least pretend to.

---

8   Felicity Barringer, "The Mainstreaming of Marxism in U.S. College," *The New York Times*, October 25, 1989, https://www.nytimes.com/1989/10/25/us/education-the-mainstreaming-of-marxism-in-us-colleges.html?fbclid=IwAR3N1H0Hr6l7fJzT5-AmMAZE5kSljxAl5Bm8KRGibJ7IY6x1FbHI-NA39T00 (accessed September 5, 2024).

They would, he wrote, get jobs at universities, in government, and at journalistic institutions, taking these places over from the inside and using their new perches to spread their ideas. In a letter to a friend, he called this "the long march through the institutions," a name that echoed the "long march" that Mao Zedong's Communist Army took during the Chinese Civil War in the 1930s. Within months, the idea was showing up in books and pamphlets distributed among left-wing groups in Europe.

But American leftists (as usual) were a little slow to catch up. In the spring of 1968, hordes of them stormed the campus of Columbia University, attempting to force the university to adopt a series of left-wing positions. They forcibly removed teachers and administrators from their offices, broke windows, and assaulted anyone who got too close. Student activists gave lessons on the quad about the work of Marxist philosophers such as Theodore Adorno and Herbert Marcuse (whom we met in the last chapter when they were palling around in Europe with guys who liked to teach kids about "free love").

Finally, after months of chaos and violence, the university caved and delivered on several of the protestors' stated goals. But the damage was done. Photographs taken that academic year—including several shots of students smoking with their feet up on the university president's desk—were plastered on the front pages of newspapers for months, and Columbia's reputation as an august Ivy League institution took a nose-dive. Donations declined. So did admissions. As the philosopher Alan Bloom put it, the incident proved that universities were "no longer places of intellectual and academic debate, but rather places of 'political correctness' and liberalism."

The public largely shared this view. In the aftermath of the protests at Columbia University, the left-wing radical groups that had been dominating the news cycles no longer seemed like harmless idiots. They seemed like dangerous psychos, willing to do anything to topple American society. Anyone who didn't think so was probably convinced that summer, when an even larger crowd of left-wing radicals attacked the site of the Democratic National Convention in Chicago. There, protestors clashed with police on the streets. And unlike today's media, which refers to protests involving the physical assault of police officers as "mostly peaceful," newspapers and major networks reported on the events accurately.

During the protests, the activists chanted "the whole world is watching." Which it was. By the end of the DNC riots, during which more than six hundred protestors were arrested and hundreds of people were injured, the left-wing terrorists had been revealed to the country for what they were. Their dreams of violent revolution had largely failed. And although the violence continued throughout the 1970s, many leaders of the neo-Marxist movement in America went underground, adopting the tactics of Rudi Dutschke and his friends on the German Left. Rather than attacking the institutions of the United States with bombs and battering rams as they'd been trying to do for years, they would *join* those institutions, trying to shape them from the inside over the next few decades. Playing the long game, in other words.

Some joined Hollywood studios. Others went into business. But the most successful became professors at American universities, whose academic freedom policies and guarantees of tenure made them the ideal places to work out half-baked, insane ideas. By the late 1980s, when Marxist governments all over the world began crumbling, they remained safe in their faculty lounges, ruminating on different ways to spread their ideology peacefully while sipping on lattes from the school cafeteria (and making big capitalist-sized salaries while they did it).

The key, many of these professors realized, was staying away from the nitty-gritty subjects like economics and hard sciences. As millions of peasant farmers in China had found out the hard way, Marxist economics and reality don't mix. What these professors *could* do, however, was mix Marxism with the softer disciplines such as English, psychology, and sociology. Although they didn't have the prestige of physics and mathematics, these subjects tended to shape how students viewed reality. Infecting these disciplines was the quickest way to infect minds at the most basic level.

For a while, this nonsense only existed on the campuses of universities. Professors would write articles, and students would have to regurgitate those articles in their papers to get good grades. Then those students would graduate, forget everything they'd heard, and move on with their lives. But as more and more left-wing nutjobs joined university faculties, these bad ideas began to stick. According to a survey conducted in 2006, more than 20 percent of American professors openly identified as "Marxist," which was about 19.9999 percent more than the number of professors willing to identify as "conservative."

Then, over the past few years, the Gen Z kids came along, and the perfect storm began to happen. Finally, a generation who'd been raised by helicopter parents to believe that the world was a dangerous, unfair place—and that they were special little angels who should never face any adversity for any reason—met a set of left-wing theories that perfectly mapped onto their view of the world. They were perfectly happy to believe that the United States was an evil, racist place that wanted to oppress sexual minorities and people of color. They were happy to call everyone they didn't like racist, and to form mobs on the quads of their colleges to shout down speakers whose ideas made them uncomfortable.

Around the same time, the number of administrators—meaning people who work at a university but do not teach—exploded. Between 1978 and 2018, according to the

Progressive Policy Institute, "full-time administrators and other professionals employed by those institutions increased by 164% and 452%, respectively."[9] For the most part, these "administrators" were hired to look after the feelings of students. They were therapists, "diversity, equity, and inclusion" (DEI) officers, and people who sat in meetings all day to ensure no one was ever offended by anything. To pay for all of them, tuition rates also skyrocketed. A private college cost about $20,000 per year in 2004; today, the same college costs almost $50,000 per year. At top-tier universities, that number is closer to $80,000. It's no surprise that after spending so much money to learn that America is evil and "white oppressors" should be violently attacked, left-wing graduates are demanding the Biden administration pay back their student loans.

In June 2023, shortly after the Supreme Court declared that the student loan forgiveness program was unconstitutional, I interviewed Sebastian Gorka on *Newsline*. He said, "I just have two words to say to all of the news in the last forty-eight hours. *President Trump*. Let's be clear. If we didn't have three originalists, nominated by President Trump, on the Supreme Court, we'd have nothing." I played a clip of Nancy Pelosi from July 2021 in which she said, "People think the president of the United States has the power for debt forgiveness. He does not. He can postpone. He can delay. But he does not have that power. That has to be an act of Congress." Sebastian Gorka concluded the segment by saying, "Well, I've lived fifty-two years on this earth and I never thought I would say this. But thank you, Nancy Pelosi."

---

9   Paul Weinstein, "How to Cut Administrative Bloat at U.S. Colleges," Progressive Policy Institute, August 17, 2023, https://www.progressivepolicy. org/pressrelease/new-report-how-to-cut-administrative-bloat-at-u-s-colleges/ (accessed September 5, 2024).

Of course, a year later, Joe Biden bragged about the fact that he was going to ignore the Supreme Court's ruling. Speaking with characteristic eloquence, Biden said, "Tens of millions of people in debt were literally about to be canceled in debts. But my MAGA Republican friends in the Congress, elected officials and special interests stepped in and sued us. And the Supreme Court blocked it. But that didn't stop me."

Today, the virus of woke neo-Marxism has escaped the lab. The convoluted academic theory of "deconstruction" has given way to plain-old destruction, as left-wing mobs run through our streets tearing down statues and occupying buildings. Even at the highest levels of government, ideas like "equity," "oppression," and "intersectionality" are treated seriously, although I doubt that the people using these terms have any idea what they really mean, or where they come from. During the summer of 2020, several works of nonsensical neo-Marxist trash made their way to the top of the best-seller lists, including *White Fragility* by the academic Robin DiAngelo and *How to Be an Antiracist* by Ibram X. Kendi.

In these books, which were read widely—or at least *bought* widely—by the general public, you'll find sentences such as "There is a collective glee in the white polity when black bodies are punished" (DiAngelo) and "The only answer to past discrimination is present discrimination" (Kendi). Ideas that were once on the far-left fringes of society are now considered mainstream. The Biden White House routinely puts out documents that reference the doctrines of critical race theory, dealing out COVID-19 aid to "communities of color" before everyone else, and ensuring that society is reshaped according to the tenets of Marxism. In the summer of 2024, it was revealed that Admiral Rachel Levine, a man in a dress with a degree from Harvard University, demanded that the minimum-age restrictions be removed from guidance about "gender-affirming care" for minors. For a normal person, this would be evil. But for a woke neo-Marxist who believes that gender is just a social construct anyway, it's all part of the job.

There was a time when people who complained about all the insane things happening on our college campuses—the riots, the shout-downs, and the refusal to see the world like adults—were told they were worrying too much. People said that college students would grow up and grow out of their radical ideas just like past generations had. But something about this generation, whether it's the constant reliance on social media or the lingering damage from their helicopter parents, has made their bad, neo-Marxist ideas stick.

And they're not going *anywhere*.

In June 2024, a left-wing mob surrounded a synagogue in Los Angeles, shattering the Sunday morning peace, threatening Jewish people as they walked into the building to worship. Once again, they chanted "from the river to the sea," and "long live intifada." Before long, the pro-Palestinian protestors incited violence, punching people and shoving them around. The people who'd once insisted that "words are violence" were now committing *actual* violence, and no one seemed to care. The headline of a CNN report filed the next day was: "Pro-Palestinian protest outside LA synagogue criticized as 'antisemitic' after street fights with pro-Israel protestors." Not surprising, from the network that ran a "mostly peaceful protests" chyron under an image of a reporter standing amid burning rubble during the summer of 2020.

Shortly after the event, I interviewed Ric Grenell, director of national intelligence under President Trump who also lived in Los Angeles at the time. He said, "I just have to say to my fellow voters in California, *What do you expect when you vote for people who want a sanctuary city and a sanctuary state?* Karen Bass, the mayor of LA, is atrocious. Things have gotten worse under her leadership. It's clear she's just a politician. She doesn't know how to lead, she doesn't know how to get out, and say forget all this progressive left-wing rhetoric. Arrest people who break the law!"

As journalist Andrew Sullivan, who resigned from his job at *New York* magazine in 2018 due to pressure from young, woke staffers, put it, "We all live on campus now." In his final column for the magazine, he wrote, "When elite universities shift their entire worldview away from liberal education as we have long known it toward the imperatives of an identity-based 'social justice' movement, the broader culture is in danger of drifting away from liberal democracy as well. If elites believe that the core truth of our society is a system of interlocking and oppressive power structures based around immutable characteristics like race or sex or sexual orientation, then sooner rather than later, this will be reflected in our culture at large."[10]

Unfortunately, this has already happened.

The unrest at our universities over the past few decades should have been a warning about what was coming. But we didn't listen. Instead, we sat back and did nothing as students graduated from elite universities, their heads full of woke, neo-Marxist nonsense, and took jobs at every corporation, media organization, and government office in the country. Today, the woke agenda is so enmeshed in our daily life that we hardly recognize it anymore. The long game—or, as the Marxists put it, the long *march*—is complete.

And the signs are everywhere.

---

10   Andrew Sullivan, "We All Live on Camus Now," *New York*, February 9, 2018, https://nymag.com/intelligencer/2018/02/we-all-live-on-campus-now.html (accessed September 5, 2024).

CHAPTER FIVE

THE WOKE AGENDA: IT'S EVERYWHERE

In the spring of 2024, as college campuses all over the country were being turned upside down by radical left-wing protestors, I entered a quiet gymnasium in suburban Massachusetts to see my daughter graduate high school. Watching her stride across the stage in her white dress, a traditional floral wreath adorning her head, my heart filled with pure joy. It was almost like watching a movie.

Then I remembered: *The world she's about to enter has gone completely insane.*

At that very moment, tents filled with violent Hamas supporters were going up at Harvard University, just a few miles from where I sat. The nuclear codes were controlled by a "well-meaning man with a poor memory," as Special Counsel Robert Hur had put it, and his predecessor (the only sane president we'd had in decades) had just been found guilty of made-up crimes by a kangaroo court in Manhattan.

But I pushed all this out of my mind. This was a day to celebrate.

After the ceremony, my daughter and I went to a Japanese restaurant near campus for selfies, sushi, and a little Saki. Minnie, one of my closest and oldest friends, joined us with her daughters. Her youngest was one of my daughter's closest friends since the fourth grade. We had marked holidays over the years with our girls and now my only and her last were leaving for college. My daughter was headed to New York to study art; her daughter would start her college journey in California that same fall. For me, it was nice to get a break from the crazy woke stuff I'd been covering on television every day.

But getting away wasn't easy.

These days, it never is.

Near the end of the brunch, my daughter's friend, with a playful look in her eye, asked Minnie if she wanted to tell us anything.

"What do you mean?" Minnie asked.

"The way you labeled the calendar invite for this reservation dinner," her daughter said. "You put *her/them* as your pronouns. That means you're gender fluid!"

"What?!"

After a few minutes of laughter, Minnie checked her phone and realized what she'd done. The option to select your own pronouns is a drop-down Apple menu. She'd assumed that the *her/them* option meant the dinner was for *her*, the mom, and *them*, the kids. But now everyone she'd sent an email over the past few days was going to think she was making some announcement.

Pass the saki, please! We may need another carafe!

At first glance, pronouns on an iPhone seem like a stupid thing to worry about. After all, who really cares? If some people want to be *they/thems* and others want to dress up like the opposite gender, that should be none of anyone's business.

But if I've learned anything covering the woke movement over the past few years, it's that nothing about it is as trivial as it seems at first.

Even the smallest things aren't small.

They're sinister.

Today, you can laugh about your friend accidentally declaring herself non-binary on her calendar app. Tomorrow, the Biden administration might make it illegal to have a dinner without at least one non-binary person present. And laughing about that person's funny clothing will be punishable by five years in federal prison. As Kamala Harris put it in a recently unearthed clip, "We have to stay woke. Like everybody needs to be woke. And you can talk about if you're the wokest or woker, but just stay more woke than less woke."[1]

Sadly, we're not far from this reality today, and it has all happened so fast.

In the years since "woke" was born on college campuses in the early '90s, this movement has overtaken nearly every segment of American life. Even at a brunch in Boston's Back Bay, it's impossible to get away from it. Today, young people graduating high school have no choice but to run up against this agenda in their daily lives. Boys and girls meet young, impressionable kids every day who believe they're gender-fluid or non-binary, and the kids are forced to assent to that reality or face the threat of cancelation. They learn a skewed, left-wing version of history, and they are forced to repeat that version of history on tests or risk failing their classes.

And it doesn't stop when kids leave high school and college. Today, the principles of diversity, equity, and inclusion (DEI) have become the norm at companies of all kinds. Bosses are forced to hire people not for their skills, but for immutable characteristics such as race, gender, and even sexual preference. I'm not sure what the interview process is like, but I'd imagine it's now common to hear things like, *I'm so sorry this*

---

1   Emma Colton, "Harris says 'everybody needs to be woke' in unearthed clip spreading like wildfire on social media," Fox News, August 5, 2024, https://www.foxnews.com/politics/harris-says-everybody-needs-woke-unearthed-clip-spreading-like-wildfire-social-media (accessed September 6, 2024).

didn't work out, ma'am, but we already have too many white women in the office. Any chance you're bisexual?

Several Democrat-run states have passed laws that would require all companies operating within the state to have women as well as members of historically marginalized groups on their boards. In the future, board meetings in California won't be able to begin until there is one woman, one gay person, one trans person, and one Native American present. And, unfortunately for Senator Elizabeth "Pocahontas" Warren, these board members will probably have to provide some documentation to prove their victimhood status.

Again, it's funny until you remember the companies we're dealing with.

Airlines, for instance.

Over the past few years, it's become increasingly common for *pilots* to be hired based on DEI criteria. As the daughter of a flight attendant, I know firsthand how important it is to have only the best people up in the sky. During her flights around the world with American Airlines, my mother worked with countless pilots, all of whom were hired solely for their ability to fly a plane. (Imagine that.) During several high-stress situations, including when severe turbulence hit and a lightning strike reverberated through the cabin, I felt comfortable knowing that she was in good hands up there. So did the hundreds of thousands of passengers who flew with her over the years.

Today, we can't be sure. According to recent guidelines, airlines are no longer interested in hiring based on ability alone. They've lowered the standards for new pilots, allowing members of so-called underrepresented groups to get a turn in the cockpit. During an interview with *Axios* in June 2021, the CEO of United Airlines, Scott Kirby, said that one of the company's main priorities would be to ensure that 50 percent of its graduating pilot classes would be women or people of color, lamenting the fact that the current number was only 19 percent.

"One of the things we do," he said, "is for every job, when we do an interview, we require women and people of color to be involved in the interview process, bringing people in early in their careers as well and giving them those opportunities… and creating a stronger bench."[2]

Shortly thereafter, it was revealed that in addition to running airlines, Kirby had a habit of dressing up in drag—including once as Taylor Swift and Lady Gaga—and dancing in flash mobs at company parties.

So, if you're reading this and you've got a flight booked on United in the near future, don't worry. You'll be in the hands of one of the most diverse crews in history. As to how good that crew will be at not crashing the airline? Who knows?! I guess you'll be one of the many people who've involuntarily signed up to be crash test dummies for the nation's wokest airline and Joe Biden's FAA.[3]

And it's not just United. Virgin Airlines also flies its freak flag proudly. In a commercial produced for the company in late 2022, just as people were beginning to get back in the skies after a pandemic-induced lull in travel, Virgin proudly asked its customers to "see the world differently." In the ad, pilots wore tongue rings, and the male flight attendant had sparkly pink eyeshadow on. Now, personally, I can't imagine a better way to keep people *out* of the skies than to let them

2   Axios, "United has 1 executive of color, but CEO is 'proud' of the diversity in his C-suite," Facebook, June 21, 2021, https://www.facebook.com/axios-news/videos/united-has-1-executive-of-color-but-ceo-is-proud-of-the-diver-sity-in-his-c-suite/357076666038400/ (accessed September 18, 2024).

3   Evan Poellinger, "Video Report: United Airlines CEO and DEI Advocate Scott Kirby Dancing in Drag to Lady Gaga," mrcTV, January 19, 2024, https://mrctv.org/blog/evan-poellinger/video-report-united-airlines-ceo-and-dei-advocate-scott-kirby-dancing-drag (accessed September 6, 2024).

know that pilots are free to be their "true selves," but I guess that's why I'm not the CEO of an airline. (Which is good, because even *I* wouldn't wear heels as high as the ones Scott Kirby sported in his infamous drag video.)

You might wonder how this ideology infected corporate America, where profit is supposed to matter more than anything else, especially given that the companies are publicly traded, and thus have a fiduciary duty to shareholders. The answer, strangely, lies with the way the radical Left has managed to infiltrate every level of these companies, especially human resources. From there, the left-wing grads we've been reading about for three chapters now enforce strange, neo-Marxist ideology on capitalists, and the capitalists smile along because they're afraid of getting canceled by their young, woke employees. This vicious cycle is the rot of corporate America.

But the pressure to go woke doesn't only come from the young left-wing foot soldiers at the bottom of the company. Lately, it also comes from the largest investment firms in the United States. In recent years, the "big three" firms—BlackRock, State Street, and Vanguard—have adopted a set of policies known as ESG, or "environmental, social, and governance." Investment decisions are made based not on how much money a company makes, but on how well (and how loudly) companies espouse left-wing talking points, and how well they're doing on their DEI goals.

And we're not talking about a little money here.

As of 2024, these three investment firms owned a majority of shares in 88 percent of the companies listed on the S&P 500, according to the *Wall Street Journal.* That means that any company you can think of—from Nike and McDonald's to Delta Airlines, Abercrombie, and Baskin Robins—are owned by these giant, ESG-loving firms. With those shares come immense power. When a CEO doesn't say the right thing in public about Black Lives Matter, for instance, BlackRock can have him fired, or lower his compensation. When a company doesn't appear to have enough transgender lesbians with purple hair on its board, State Street can threaten to make life hard for everyone at the company until this mistake is remedied. If you find yourself wondering why Delta Airlines is beginning to forego the phrase "ladies and gentlemen" during gate announcements, wonder no longer. It's all about pleasing the woke private equity overlords.

One of the tools these firms use to enforce their will is called a Corporate Equality Index Score, or "CEI Score" for short. This score is given out by an LGBTQIA+ political activist group called the Human Rights Campaign. According to a recent report in the *New York Post*, this group has "received millions from George Soros' Open Society Foundation," which has also funneled cash into other left-wing causes across the United States. Every year, the Human Rights Campaign (which is currently run by Kelley Robinson, a former political organizer for Barack Obama) issues report cards to American companies, grading them on how well they're adhering to woke ideology. The five major criteria, according to the *Post*, are "'Workforce Protections,' 'Inclusive Benefits,' 'Supporting an Inclusive Culture,' 'Corporate Social Responsibility,' and 'Responsible Citizenship.' A company can lose CEI points if it doesn't fulfill HRC's demand for 'integration of intersectionality in professional development, skills-based or other training,' or if it doesn't use a 'supplier diversity program with demonstrated effort to include certified LGBTQ+ suppliers.'"

So, let's say you start a make-up company. You produce great products, make lots of money, and treat your employees like kings and queens. After a few years, your company goes public, and a company like BlackRock buys 10 percent of your shares. Then BlackRock finds out that you've had the nerve to get the plastic for your lipstick tubes from people who *aren't even gay*! In today's upside-down business world, that'll cost you.

Big time.

It's no wonder they call these people, who have added so many letters to *LGBTQ(IA)+* that it's starting to look like the password on the back of a Wi-Fi router, "the Alphabet Mafia." That's exactly how they act. They bully, intimidate, and force people into submission. And somehow, they've been able to do it to the leaders of our nation's largest companies—who, we've been told for years, are bloodsucking capitalist monsters who don't care about anything but profit. They've managed to do this not because their cause is just or because their ideology makes any sense at all, but because the CEOs are all terrified of what'll happen to them if they don't play ball. So, when the latest list of nutty demands comes in from HRC, the CEOs go ahead and implement it, knowing their jobs are always on the line.

The annual list of demands might as well say, "Nice company. It'd be a shame if anything…*happened* to it."

Of course, you might be wondering again whether this is such a big deal. After all, "diversity," "equity," and "inclusion" don't sound like bad words. When most people hear them, they probably think the company is just trying to include all different kinds of people, because including all kinds of different people is probably good for business. At least that's what we've been told since 2015, when consulting firm McKinsey declared that after an extensive study, analysts at the company had found definitive proof that racial and gender diversity led to higher profits for companies. As a recent report in the *Wall Street Journal* points out, this study was "a breakthrough" when it first came out. Over the years, the research was "used by investors, lobbyists, and regulators to push for more women and minority groups on boards, and to justify investing in companies that appointed them."

The problem?

It wasn't true.

"Since 2015," according to the *Journal*'s findings, published in June 2024, "the approach has been tested in the fire of the marketplace and failed. Academics have tried to repeat McKinsey's findings and failed, concluding that there is in fact no link between profitability and executive diversity. And the methodology of McKinsey's early studies, which helped create the widespread belief that diversity is good for profits, is being questioned."[4]

Once again, "researchers" with liberal biases have published the findings they *wished* were true, not the ones that actually *are* true. The most ridiculous part, of course, is that these findings should have been obvious to anyone with a little common sense. There is no reason to believe that having a certain number of people from different racial and sexual backgrounds in a boardroom should have any effect at all on how much money a company makes. Why would it? Best case scenario, spending all day worrying about nonsense like that will result in no change at all to corporate profits or shareholder value.

Worst case scenario, all that worrying about how many Native Americans, bisexuals, and trans people you have in your boardroom is going to seriously affect the quality of your products—or your customer service, or your research and development, or some other area of the company you can't even think about because you're too busy trying to track down equitable suppliers to make George Soros happy.

Sadly, this is already happening to many companies.

---

4   James Mackintosh, "Diversity Was Supposed to Make Us Rich. Not So Much," *The Wall Street Journal*, June 28, 2024, https://www.wsj.com/finance/investing/diversity-was-supposed-to-make-us-rich-not-so-much-39da6a23?st=v3qqv6hqjmk4yfl&reflink=article_copyURL_share (accessed September 6, 2024).

In early 2023, for instance, Alissa Heinerscheid, the new head of marketing at Bud Light—whose parent company, AB InBev, is owned in part by BlackRock and Vanguard—announced that she was going to make some big changes at the company. The brand's image, she said, was "out of touch," and "fratty." So, she and her team tracked down Dylan Mulvaney, a young man who'd begun his "transition journey" by dressing and speaking like a thirteen-year-old girl, and sent him a beer can with his picture on it. Shortly thereafter, Mulvaney posted a photo of himself in a bubble bath, sipping from a can of Bud Light.

Now, I'm not a huge fan of light beer myself. But I know plenty of people who love it. And most of *those* people have a sense of humor that Alissa Heinerscheid would probably find "out of touch" and "fratty." Meaning that when they saw a skinny man with lipstick giggling in a bubble bath about his "365 days of girlhood," they found it ridiculous. And gross. Unlike the tiny, *tiny* percentage of Americans who do suffer from gender dysphoria, Dylan Mulvaney did not want to become a woman his own age. He wanted to become a prepubescent girl, signaling that there was something deeply off about him. Watching him prance around the Plaza Hotel dressed as the children's book character Eloise, it's impossible not to get the creeps. Which millions of Americans, hearing the news that this person was now the spokesperson for their favorite beer, did.

In April 2023, I spoke with Brianna Lyman, a reporter at the *Daily Caller*, who said, "Here's the thing. Bud Light. Do they not know who their demographic is? Because I can tell you, the guys I know who drink Bud Light, they certainly don't care about transgender activism.… If we're looking at the scope of women's history during women's history month, real women are under attack! We're being subjected to mockery by men who dress up and put makeup on and grow their hair out. We have been reduced down to nothing but appearances, and that is certainly not what women are.... And you have companies that are perpetuating that narrative."

In the weeks following the announcement, Bud Light's consumer base revolted. Kid Rock shot a stack of Bud Light cans in his backyard. Ordinary Americans filmed themselves dumping their kegs into rivers, and social media lit up with denunciations of the new ad campaign. The company, which had counted on the social approval it gained from buying into the latest woke fad to carry it through the controversy, couldn't stop the bleeding fast enough. By June 2023, just two months after the brand announced its partnership with Dylan Mulvaney, AB InBev had lost $27 billion in market value, including a 4 percent drop in the stock during the first week of June. The "middle men," meaning the hardworking delivery guys and mom-and-pop retailers who sell Bud Light all over the country, were also hit hard—all because one person at the company wanted to appease a bunch of woke idiots.

The VP of marketing who came up with the scheme lost her job, and the rest of the executive team learned that there was only so far you could shove a wacky agenda down your customers' throats before they had enough. Since the incident, the brand has gone back to its roots, bringing back the Clydesdales and partnering with popular comedians in an attempt to undo some of the damage. But, in business, this kind of thing is hard to forget. Once customers learn that you care more about pleasing woke idiots and a bunch of shadowy figures at the top of the nation's largest investment firms more than you care about selling them good products, it's hard to get their trust back.

And it's not just Bud Light. Over the past few years, the phrase "Go woke, go broke" has found its way into coverage of the corporate world. Lately, companies have begun to realize that when they support causes that are antithetical to the beliefs of the people who buy their products or use their services, they're going to get themselves in trouble. It's happened to the outdoor brand Patagonia, whose CEO put out a statement claiming that the outdoors was "racist." It's happened to Major League Baseball, which moved its All-Star Game out of Georgia to protest Voter ID laws and was met with huge boycotts and protests as a result. The tide is turning.

Of course, the worst that happened to these companies was a dip in profits. A few people lost their jobs, and the share price suffered for a few months. But that's only the tip of the iceberg. Sometimes, when companies focus on nonsense rather than making sure they're making good products, the outcome is much worse.

Sometimes, people die.

The plane left the ground in Portland, Oregon, around five o'clock in the evening, climbing slowly toward its cruising altitude. The 177 passengers onboard were bound for Ontario, California. It was January 5, 2024.

Flight attendants walked up and down the aisles, settling in for an easy, two-hour trip. The "fasten seatbelts" sign was on. The cabin lights were dim. Then, just as the lights of Portland were beginning to fade into the night, the left side of the plane creaked.

Something went *pop*.

One passenger, a young woman, looked to her left.

A chunk of the plane was missing.

As freezing wind blew into the cabin, passengers huddled in their seats. Fathers held young children, likely wondering if this would be the last time they'd ever be able to do so. In videos of the incident, scattered screams can barely be heard over the sound of the wind. Watching the video, I couldn't help wondering how many people onboard knew anything about the aircraft they were sitting on. The plane, which said Alaska Airlines on the side, was a 737 Max, produced by Boeing.

Shortly after the incident, I interviewed a survivor on *Newsline*. The man, who had been seated just behind the door plug that gave out during the flight, spoke about the harrowing ordeal, saying, "The door was already gone, the air started rushing in, extremely fast, extremely loud, and extremely cold. It was very terrifying.... I thought we were going to die as the hole was so big."

Five years earlier, two of these airplanes had crashed due to mechanical failures, killing all 346 passengers. In the aftermath of these horrific disasters, the heads of Boeing had promised to make changes at the company—the kind that would ensure that no disasters of this kind ever happened again. I watched these developments closely, remembering what it was like to sit at home looking out the window while my mother was up in the sky on her way to some foreign country, safe in the knowledge that all staff onboard knew what they were doing. Back then, I felt certain that only the best people were allowed to fly airplanes, and that all necessary safety precautions had been taken. It didn't occur to me to think otherwise.

Today, I'm not so sure. I have serious doubts about the people and the planes. In the aftermath of the two high-profile crashes, Boeing made some changes at the corporate level. But not the ones most people were hoping for. A CEO was fired, and a few other people were brought on, very few of whom had any direct experience in the airline or manufacturing industry.

In 2022, according to a recent SEC filing, "the aircraft manufacturer changed its incentive plan from giving executives bonuses based on passenger safety, employee safety, and quality to rewarding them if they hit climate and DEI targets."[5] Around the same time, as the *New York Post* pointed out, Boeing issued a "'Global Equity, Diversity & Inclusion 2023 Report,' which noted that 'also in 2022, for the first time in our company's history, we tied incentive compensation to inclusion'...'Our goal was to achieve diverse interview slates for at least 90 percent of manager and executive openings,' the report said, adding that the company exceeded the target, 'with 92 percent of interview slates being diverse, resulting in 47 percent diverse hires.'"

Well, great job, Boeing.

But I don't think the people shivering in their seats, wondering if they were about to get sucked out of the plane and tossed into the black skies above Portland cared very much that Boeing's C-suite finally had George Soros's preferred number of gender-queer polyamorous people in it. I think they were probably a little more concerned about the bolts that had just come loose on the side panel of the plane.

Fortunately, Alaska Airlines Flight 1282 was able to circle back and land with all 177 of its passengers alive and well, if a little shaken and traumatized (and not just because they'd landed back in the woke wasteland of Portland, Oregon). The incident with the door panel was a stark reminder that in modern America, companies cannot be relied upon to keep us safe. When a shady overseas activist group tells them to change the composition of their boards and spout woke talking points, they get on it right away. When Congress and the American people ask them to keep planes from falling apart in the skies, however, the results are a little more mixed. That same month, two more Boeing 737 Max planes had "incidents" in the sky, rapidly losing altitude and resulting in

---

5   Shannon Thaler, "Boeing prioritizing diversity and inclusion over flier safety, Elon Musk says after near-catastrophic Alaska Airlines mishap" *New York Post,* January 11, 2024, https://nypost.com/2024/01/11/business/elon-musk-rips-boeing-they-prioritized-dei-over-safety/ (accessed September 6, 2024).

injuries to more than twenty people onboard. The American public demanded answers.

One of them came from an employee at Boeing, who spoke to Christopher Rufo of *City Journal* on the condition of anonymity. According to this employee, the company's focus on left-wing causes like DEI had directly impacted its ability to ensure that all planes were safe.

"At its core," says the whistleblower, "we have a marginalization of the people who build stuff, the people who really work on these planes."[6] While the executives flew around in private jets and worked from their homes in New Hampshire, Connecticut, and Florida, focusing on keeping investors happy with the company's performance on nonsensical metrics like DEI, the facilities where airplanes are manufactured and fixed suffered immensely.

"If you look at the bumper stickers at the factories in Renton or Everett," according to the whistleblower, "it's a lot of conservative people who like building things—and conservative people do not like politics at work."[7] He also points out that unlike tech companies, which can afford to pay high salaries while pursuing money-losing DEI policies, legacy companies like Boeing can't do the same thing. "Because [Google] is paying 30 or 40 percent more than the competition in salary, they are going to get the top 5 percent of whatever racial group they want. They can afford, in a sense, to pay the 'DEI tax' and still find top people." But if Boeing does the same thing, "you are going to end up with the bottom 20 percent of the preferred population."

In the aftermath of the crash, Elon Musk—who knows a thing or two about building things that fly—tweeted: "Do

---

6   Christopher F. Rufo, "'It's an Empty Executive Suite,'" *City Journal*, April 3, 2024, https://www.city-journal.org/article/insider-explains-what-has-gone-wrong-with-boeing (accessed September 6, 2024).

7   Ibid.

you want to fly in an airplane where they prioritized DEI hiring over safety? That is actually happening."

In response, he was lambasted by the Left as a racist and a conspiracy theorist.

During an interview with Musk for his short-lived show on X, former CNN host Don Lemon tied himself in knots trying to paint his new boss as a racist for telling the truth about the dangers of DEI.

"There's no evidence of that, Elon," he said.

But maybe Don has a point. Maybe it's just a coincidence that after decades without a single serious incident, Boeing planes began malfunctioning in the sky at exactly the same time that ESG, DEI, and social activism took over corporate America. Maybe the fact that American companies now need to devote an enormous portion of their resources to making BlackRock and left-wing activist groups happy really has *nothing* to do with the fact that they're beginning to slip up in other places.

On the other hand, sometimes the simplest explanation is the correct one. Usually, the media has no trouble understanding this. Whenever something goes wrong with a SpaceX rocket, for instance, we're inundated by the mainstream media with think pieces about how the real cause of the mechanical failure is Elon Musk's "toxic masculinity," or "right-wing political leanings." Whenever anything bad happens to a non-white person in the United States, we're told that "white supremacy," an impossibly broad category that encompasses anything that liberals don't like, is responsible.

But when a company radically alters its incentive structure and operational procedures virtually overnight, the legacy media throw up their collective hands and say, *Gee, we wonder why things at the company are falling apart!* The answer, as usual, is staring them right in the face. They just don't want to see it.

Consider, for instance, that in June 2024, two astronauts aboard a spacecraft manufactured by Boeing got stuck in space. Just *stuck*, floating miles above the atmosphere with no way to get back down. I'm sure you can imagine how the mainstream media would have covered this if it was a SpaceX rocket, rather than one built by Boeing for the federal government, that left two astronauts stranded in space. We'd have had endless cable news coverage of how the astronauts were doing, live coverage of their ship in orbit, and rants from left-wing hosts about how Elon Musk represents everything that's wrong with cis, heterosexual white capitalist men.

But since the company in question happened to be onboard with all the same liberal causes as the media, we heard nothing. The *New York Times* ran a headline deep in its science section reading "Astronauts Are Not Stuck on the I.S.S., NASA and Boeing Officials Say." Around the same time, *Scientific American* ran one stating that the astronauts were "stuck, but safe in space."

You know, space? That endless black void in which no life can exist?

Well, it turns out, you can be "stuck, but safe" there as long as the company that put you there has a diverse enough board.

As of this writing, Elon Musk has offered to get the astronauts back. But he's been rebuffed at every turn. Best estimates say that the astronauts will spend more than eight months in space! I hope that by the time this book reaches your hands, we'll know that they'll be able to return home safely.

Thankfully, the problems at Boeing have been exposed. But consider the fact that small slip-ups at Boeing—loose screws in planes, faulty thrusters on rocket ships—can cause giant catastrophes. The problem, as the whistleblower who spoke to Chris Rufo pointed out, is that similar failures are probably happening at companies all over the country, in every sector of the economy. We just haven't noticed yet because *those* slip-ups don't make planes fall out of the sky. But sooner or later, even the coverage of the legacy media won't be enough to hide the fact that DEI and "woke-enomics" has been a disaster for the United States.

Now, I'm not saying that diversity is a bad thing. When I got my first job at a news station in the early '90s, for instance, it wasn't nearly as common as it is today for young women to work in the business. Most were much older. But I didn't get that job because someone told my future boss that he needed to hire more women or risk losing funding. I didn't get it because I put "Hispanic woman" right at the top of my resume. I got it because I worked hard and got my work in front of every last station manager on the East Coast who would take a meeting with me. The fact that I happened to be female and Hispanic was a bonus.

Which, as it turns out, is how these things tend to work. When you hire only the best people, you'll end up getting a diverse employee base as a natural side effect. In fact, the only thing we *did* learn from the botched McKinsey study about diversity, according to the *Wall Street Journal*, is that "profitability [leads] to diversity, not the other way around."[8] Luckily, some state and local governments around the country have taken proactive steps to end DEI and wokeness in hiring.

In January 2024, Texas implemented new laws that restrict DEI programs in publicly funded institutions, including banning mandatory DEI training and prohibiting public entities from organizing programs that mandate such training. Around the same time, Arizona passed legislation preventing public universities and community colleges from requiring DEI statements from job applicants and limiting the implementation of DEI programs in state-funded institutions.

---

8   Mackintosh, "Diversity Was Supposed to Make Us Rich."

In a sane world, the federal government would have gotten the memo, too. But in the Biden administration, which has been overrun by young woke radicals since Joe Biden was still campaigning from his basement, DEI remains all the rage. Without it, Kamala Harris would still be cackling away in California somewhere rather than out on the campaign trail running for president. But Joe Biden, needing to please the young and the woke, promised that he would nominate his vice president based not on experience, but on the immutable characteristics of race and gender. Now he's skulking around the White House in silence, and she's out spouting her typically impenetrable drivel to crowds all over the country.

This woke stuff, in other words, isn't going anywhere.

Not until Joe Biden and Kamala Harris—and crackhead Hunter Biden, who was apparently prepping his father for interviews—get out of the White House for good.

From the moment that Joe Biden and his goons took office, the woke agenda has been spreading like wildfire. Today, there's no area of public life that isn't infected.

Rather than addressing the serious problems with air travel, for instance, the Biden administration nominated yet *another* DEI-friendly pick named Phillip Washington who happened to be a friend of several key Democrats in Colorado. The job (which entails overseeing all the airplanes in the country—a big responsibility, given that they seem to be breaking down in mid-air quite often lately) suddenly became a political patronage position under the Biden regime. Fortunately, Washington was pulled before his confirmation could even come to a vote in the Senate after a disastrous outing and grilling on Capitol Hill.

But some of the damage has already been done. I don't think anyone feels secure, for instance, with "Mayor" Pete Buttigieg as the secretary of transportation. Again, we see what happens when someone is selected for a job not based on skill, but on fealty to the Biden administration and sexual preference. Instead of getting to work on our crumbling infrastructure or trying to stop trains from going off the rails, Secretary Buttigieg has decided to tackle racism in our—

(Checks notes)

—roads?

Speaking from the White House briefing room in November 2021, Secretary Buttigieg unveiled his plan to "address racist highway design," saying, "If an underpass was constructed such that a bus carrying mostly Black and Puerto Rican kids to a beach…in New York was designed too low for it to pass by, that…obviously reflects racism that went into those design choices…I don't think we have anything to lose by confronting that simple reality and I think we have everything to gain by acknowledging it."[9]

Since then, we've had *thirteen* major train derailments, one of which killed three people. A bridge in Baltimore collapsed, killing six and injuring many others. A train derailment in East Palestine, Ohio, released toxic chemicals into the air and water, leading to a widespread environmental crisis and forcing the evacuation of thousands of residents. Over a holiday weekend in 2021, flights were grounded due to mechanical failures, and Secretary Buttigieg couldn't deal with it because he was on parental leave with his husband as their surrogate welcomed twins. There are people in the country who can take two months off without the world falling

9   Yacob Reyes, "Buttigieg: Infrastructure bill to address racist highway design," Axios, November 8, 2021, https://www.axios.com/2021/11/09/buttigieg-infrastructure-bill-racist-highway-design (accessed September 6, 2024).

apart. The transportation secretary isn't one of them. When *that* guy isn't on the job, the world can *literally* fall apart. Of course, if he even *was* there, would he know what to do? From the minute he took the job, the only thing he's shown that he knows how to do is cosplay like a construction worker during press conferences.

Since taking office in January 2021, the Biden administration has been laser-focused on woke nonsense (but only between the hours of 10 a.m. and 4 p.m., when the president could focus). Unfortunately, though, you can do quite a lot of damage in a six-hour day. For instance, in the first year of his term, Joe Biden did a complete (and unlawful) rewrite of Title IX, the guidelines which, among other things, set the rules governing female sports. According to this rewrite, men who claimed to be women were now considered women. All they had to do was "identify" as such, and they would be granted full access to female-only bathrooms, locker rooms, and other spaces.

Which kinds of ruins the whole "female-only" thing, when you think about it.

When Title IX was first enacted in 1972, only three hundred thousand young women played high school and college sports in the United States. Thanks to Title IX, which mandated that institutions devote equal resources to men's and women's sports, more than three million girls compete in high school sports today, and more than two hundred thousand compete in college sports. Girls are able to get athletic scholarships at rates that would have been impossible in the '70s, and they have opportunities to excel in sports that would previously have been unimaginable. The creation of leagues in which women can compete against other women have allowed millions of girls to play sports who simply wouldn't be able to if woman-only spaces didn't exist.

Today, the Biden-Harris administration is trying to say that the category of "woman" does not exist. If *all people* can say they're women—even when they have penises and beards—then no one is really a woman anymore. It's no wonder that Supreme Court Justice Ketanji Brown Jackson couldn't provide a simple definition of the word during her confirmation hearings, despite being asked for one many times. According to the woke doctrine she believes in, women don't exist.

The world saw exactly what this might look like in practice when Lia Thomas, who'd been ranked 462nd when he swam on the men's team at the University of Pennsylvania, jumped in the pool with a bunch of young women and started smashing records. All of a sudden, thanks to his superior bone structure and giant shoulder muscles, he was blowing these women out of the water—calling himself a woman while he did it. Anyone who pointed out that he was still a man was called "transphobic" and "hateful" by the mainstream media.

In 2024, I interviewed Riley Gaines, who lost a trophy to Lia Thomas. Speaking about the White House's recent event that purported to "honor" female NCAA athletes, she said, "No woman should feel supported by this administration. What this administration is actively trying to do is erase women—not just female athletes, but they're trying to erase women! Their proposed rewrite of Title IX is an abomination to what was beneficial for so many women, including my grandma's generation. They've seen these benefits and now they see that being taken away. So, make no mistake: the message that they're really sending to women like myself is that we don't matter. Our safety and our privacy and our equal opportunities, they don't matter."

Luckily, the Supreme Court saw how ridiculous these newly rewritten rules were and struck them down on April 17, 2024, enraging the gender activists at the White House.

In response to the decision, the Biden administration vowed to "keep fighting" and to pursue other legal avenues to implement its policy changes.

Clearly, there is nothing these people love more than catering to strange, mentally disturbed people (otherwise known as their voters). It makes you wonder why, in the lead-up to the 2020 election, so many commentators in the corporate media referred to Biden and his campaign as the "adults in the room." In June 2024, just after the Biden-Harris administration had the trans activist and *Queer Eye for the Straight Guy* star Jonathan Van Ness over to the White House for a visit, I spoke with Seb Gorka, former deputy assistant to President Trump, about what he thought of the spectacle.

"I am told the adults are back," he said. "Well, what I see are perverts and freaks. When we were in the White House, we got things done. We were so energy independent, we had to export it. We had the biggest economy in history. The lowest unemployment for women in seventy years. And what has all this been replaced with? Parodies of women with fake breasts unveiling them on the White House lawn? Men with beards in dresses? If we had seen this in a television show like *The West Wing* years ago, we'd have said no. There's no way that's happening in America. But it's happening right now!"

To put a cherry on top, we would later learn that the transgender person who came to the White House also happened to be the hairdresser of none other than Dylan Mulvaney! There should really be a six-degrees-of-separation game when it comes to these gender-fluid weirdos and the White House.

And speaking of cherries. At the very moment that Seb Gorka was speaking to me, the White House had just promoted a communications aide named Tyler Cherry, who had a habit of dressing in women's clothing and tweeting about how American police forces were really just modern-day "slave patrols." In 2014, he tweeted, "Cheersing in bars to ending the occupation of Palestine—no shame and fuck your glares #ISupportGaza #FreePalestine."[10] A few years earlier, Sam Brinton—another Biden official who liked wearing women's clothing to work—was caught stealing suitcases at airports and then *wearing the stolen clothing* to events around DC.

And yet in the early summer of 2024, *New York* magazine had the nerve to ask on its cover story "Are Republican Women Okay?"

Please.

As I said on the air, this comes from the same people who can't even *define* what a woman is! Rachel Levine, the trans person who says that kids can go through the wrong puberty, gets a pass from these people. So does columnist E. Jean Carroll, who said on CNN that "most people think of rape as being sexy." On the Left, they are laughing. But conservative women are not. These are serious times, and the country needs serious people.

Clearly, the adults are not in the room.

Adults would ensure that our military is the strongest and most lethal it's ever been, especially since Democrats seem to have a habit of involving the United States in a new foreign war about every six minutes. But the Biden administration has even remade the *military* according to the rules of DEI, allowing people like General Mark Milley to set the agenda. You might remember Milley, who bragged (falsely) about thwarting President Trump's will during his final days in office and said it was important that he understand Karl Marx, Mao Zedong, Lenin, and "white rage." *That* is the kind of person we have running the army—the kind who hunts down terrorists and keeps American citizens safe from harm.

---

10   Elisenne Stoller, "Biden turns up the heat on *Dobbs* anniversary," *The Spectator,* June 24, 2024, https://thespectator.com/newsletter/biden-turns-up-the-heat-on-dobbs-anniversary-dc-diary-06-24-2024/ (accessed September 7, 2024).

As usual, it began with President Barack Obama. In 2015, the Obama administration ignored warnings from the United States Marines that "gender integrated combat formations did not move as quickly or shoot as accurately, and that women were twice as likely as men to suffer combat injuries," reports Thomas Spoehr, former director of the Center for National Defense at the Heritage Foundation.[11] That same year, the Obama administration lowered the standards for physical fitness in the military. It also attempted to change the rules about transgender people serving in the military.

During the Trump administration, many of these policies were reversed. Right from the beginning, President Trump re-instituted the ban on transgender individuals, which makes sense given that they have higher rates of anxiety, depression, and a higher risk of suicide due to higher susceptibility to mental illness, as many scientific studies have shown. The priority for President Trump and members of his administration—the real "adults in the room"—was making sure that our military could, you know, *fight wars* (which is interesting, looking back, since they managed not to start any new ones during their four years in office).

But Joe Biden, of course, destroyed all that. As soon as he took office, the process for reinstituting trans soldiers began. The higher-ups at military training facilities were told they had to begin teaching neo-Marxist and anti-racist books along with their texts about military strategy, including Ibram X. Kendi's *How to Be an Antiracist*. So, rather than shooting enemy combatants like the evil, white supremacist armies of yesterday, the military under Joe Biden will hold DEI seminars for members

---

11   Thomas Spoehr, "The Rise of Wokeness in the Military," Hilldale College *Imprimis*, Vol. 51. No. 6/7 (June/July 2022), https://shop.hillsdale.edu/products/the-rise-of-wokeness-in-the-military-thomas-spoehr (accessed September 7, 2024).

of Islamist terror groups, asking them to atone for their "white supremacist adjacent" rage…which, now that I'm thinking about, might actually be worse than getting shot at.

In August 2022, soldiers stationed at Ramstein Air Base in Germany learned that the military had scheduled a "drag queen story hour" for their children, which was only canceled after a few Republican members of Congress found out about it and wrote letters to the secretary of the Air Force demanding an explanation.[12] In November 2022, pictures appeared online of several soldiers wearing "dog bondage" masks in front of an American flag. According to a description in *USA Today*, the photos depict "male soldiers in uniform, or parts of uniforms, wearing dog masks, leather and chains. Some of the photos depict poses of submission and sexual acts. Another photo shows a soldier in combat fatigues wearing the dog mask on an airfield."[13]

Although the military launched an investigation immediately, I wouldn't hold my breath waiting for the perpetrators of this strange crime to be punished. The Biden administration probably just wants to know who these people are so it can award the BDSM sex freaks Medals of Honor.

Yet no matter how much the Biden administration and the corporate media attempt to cover up the damage that a "woke military" will do to our country, the truth is going to come out. In July 2024, the Arizona State University Center for American Institutions released an eighty-page study that "calls for an immediate end to the Pentagon's multimillion-dollar

---

12 Ibid.
13 Tom Vanden Brook, "Photos of dog-masked soldiers in bondage gear while in uniform under investigation," *USA Today*, December 12, 2022, https://www.usatoday.com/story/news/politics/2022/12/12/sexually-explicit-photos-soldiers-investigation/10881795002/ (accessed September 7, 2024).

DEI bureaucracy."[14] The report, which details exactly how the military is wasting taxpayer money on woke causes, found that "there are far more effective ways to promote unity and respect among military ranks than by spending millions annually to divide servicemembers by their gender or race."[15] It also detailed concrete steps the military establishment could take to undo this damage.

Unfortunately, there's quite a lot of damage to undo, and it's not only in the military. Every organization the Biden-Harris administration touches becomes woke overnight. In 2021, the CIA posted a video starring various young, left-wing staffers. One of them says she's a "cisgender millennial" who refuses to "internalize misguided patriarchal ideas of what a woman can or should be."[16] In January 2024, it was reported that the FBI's new DEI standards had led to cases of agents who are "so fat and unfit" that they "can't even pass the new relaxed standards for fitness; who are illiterate and need remedial English lessons; who don't want to work weekends or after hours; have serious disabilities or mental-health issues, and 'create drama.'"

Keep in mind, we give these people guns.

And we rely on them for "intelligence."

When even the people who are supposed to defend this country with force go woke, we are in serious trouble. As I write these words in the summer of 2024, President Biden

---

14   Brian Freeman, "Study: 'Vast DEI Bureaucracy' in DOD Harms Military," Newsmax, July 2, 2024, https://www.newsmax.com/newsfront/military-study-dei/2024/07/02/id/1171031/ (accessed September 7, 2024).

15   Ibid.

16   Thom Waite, "The CIA's latest 'woke washing' recruitment ad stars a gay agency librarian," Dazed Digital, May 12, 2021, https://www.dazeddigital.com/life-culture/article/52759/1/the-cia-latest-woke-washing-recruitment-ad-stars-a-gay-agency-librarian (accessed September 7, 2024).

is asleep at the wheel, and we've seen the consequences of his negligence. We saw it during the disastrous pullout from Afghanistan, the increasing tension in the Middle East, and, finally, at the first presidential debate in June 2024. Nowhere has this been more apparent than our southern border, which effectively doesn't exist anymore.

And *that*, perhaps more than anything else, will soon lead to the downfall of this nation unless we do something about it.

We're running out of time.

CHAPTER SIX

SOVEREIGNTY, AND HOW TO LOSE IT

*T*hat number can't be right, I thought. *Too many zeroes.* I was sitting in my studio, preparing to go on air and deliver a report about how much money Mexican drug cartels had made per year since Joe Biden took office. There, in the research materials in front of me, was the figure $13,000,000,000.

That's thirteen *billion* dollars.

With a *b.*

There's an old saying about the difference between a million and a billion dollars, which many people (including me) have trouble fathoming. A million seconds, the saying goes, is eleven days. A *billion* seconds, on the other hand, is roughly thirty-two years. And under the open-borders policies of Joe Biden and the Democrats, the cartels have made a billion dollars *thirteen times over.* Shockingly, that number is up from just $500 million in 2018, when President Trump was in office.[1]

Now, I've always been pretty bad at math. But even *I* know that an increase from $500 million to $13 billion doesn't just come out of nowhere. It has happened because Joe Biden and

---

1 Miriam Jordan, "Smuggling Migrants at the Border Now a Billion-Dollar Business," *The New York Times,* July 25, 2022, https://www.nytimes.com/ 2022/07/25/us/migrant-smuggling-evolution.html (accessed September 7, 2024).

"border czar" Kamala Harris have rolled out the welcome mat at our southern border, creating unprecedented opportunities for the cartels to make money.

Thirteen billion dollars of money, to be exact.

Roughly twenty-six times what they were making just six years ago, when President Trump was in office.

Am I belaboring the point?

I mean to.

When it comes to the border crisis, I worry that Americans have become numb to the giant numbers we seem to hear every day.

For instance: In 2019, two years before Joe Biden took office, there were about 1.4 million "encounters" between Border Patrol and illegal immigrants. The next year, thanks to President Trump's strict border policies, that number fell to about 700,000. Then, beginning in January 2021, when Joe Biden took office, promising to welcome illegal immigrants with open arms, that number began climbing.

And *climbing*.

In 2021, there were more than 2 million encounters. In 2022, there were 3 million. In 2023, there were 3.5 million. By the time President Biden, in a desperate attempt to salvage his flailing reelection campaign, made a half-hearted attempt to secure *some* of the border via executive order in June 2024, there had been a grand total of 7.4 million recorded encounters between Border Patrol and illegal immigrants at our southwestern border.

And even *that* number doesn't tell the full story. According to Mark Morgan, the former acting commissioner of US Customs and Border Protection under President Trump (and a frequent guest on *Newsline*), the total number of migrants who've made their way into the United States under Joe Biden's watch might be as high as thirteen million. Unlike the legacy media's numbers, that one includes the "got-aways," the

Border Patrol's term for illegals who enter the United States and evade the processing border patrol agents. But with the information that Donald Trump has, he says that the number is between fifteen million and twenty million.

"What's really important is the got-aways," Morgan said during an interview with Newsmax in October 2022. "We know that there are murderers, rapists, pedophiles, gang members, and we know there are potential terrorist threats among the got-aways."

Not that things are much better with the ones who *are* detained. Under Joe Biden, those people are issued citations, given court dates (often years in the future), and allowed to roam the interior of the United States. All we can do is hope that they show up to court. Which, given that they've already broken the law by entering this country illegally, there's zero indication that they will show up in court. In fact, a recent report shows that only about 50 percent of illegal immigrants who are released into the United States are ever heard from again.[2] And many of these illegal immigrants have had help from Joe Biden and other Democrats to *get* to the interior of the United States.

In May 2024, Todd Bensman, author of *Overrun: How Joe Biden Unleashed the Greatest Border Crisis in U.S. History*, found that the Biden administration had secretly authorized flights carrying hundreds of thousands of immigrants into forty-five US cities, keeping this information hidden from the public and local authorities. This outrageous revelation, confirmed by the House Homeland Security Committee, shows the extent to which the administration bypassed transparency and accountability. Bensman highlighted that the highest

---

2   US Department of Justice, Executive Office for Immigration Review, "Adjudication Statistics," October 12, 2023, https://www.justice.gov/eoir/page/file/1153866/dl (accessed September 7, 2024).

number of immigrants was sent to Florida—over 326,000—while local leaders were left in the dark about the scale of these operations, unable to prepare or respond adequately.[3]

Democrats will tell us that this isn't a problem. And if you say it *is* a problem, they'll tell you that you're a racist. The Biden-Harris administration, along with its allies in the corporate media, hopes that when the American people hear the numbers they've just been given, their eyes will glaze over, and they won't be able to grasp the enormity of our situation.

But things are more dire than they've ever been.

I know, because I cover this crisis every day.

In the period between March 2024 and June 2024, more than four hundred unaccompanied minors *per day* have crossed the border, many of them smuggled by Mexican drug cartels for huge sums of money. According to Doctors Without Borders, 30 percent of women who make this crossing are sexually assaulted on the journey—and that's before they get to the cartel stash houses here in the United States, where many women are further sex trafficked. This is a humanitarian crisis unfolding in real time, and most left-leaning media organizations pay no attention to it simply because the facts are inconvenient for their narrative.

Under the Biden-Harris administration, the situation has gotten so bad that even liberal reporters have been forced to confront it. In a recent piece for *The Atlantic*, reporter David Leonhardt examined the stalemate that we've reached in this country around illegal immigration. "The Democratic Party," he writes, "has struggled to articulate an immigration policy

---

3   Todd Bensman, "A Secret Finally Revealed: Americans Can Know the U.S. Cities Receiving Hundreds of Thousands of Immigrants Flying from Abroad," Center for Immigration Studies, May 1, 2024, https://cis.org/Bensman/Secret-Finally-Revealed-Americans-Can-Know-US-Cities-Receiving-Hundreds-Thousands (accessed September 7, 2024).

beyond what might be summarized as: *More is better, and less is racist.*"[4]

Well, it's good to see that they're finally catching on to the fact that this is unsustainable.

And if we *allow* it to continue, more people are going to die, and the cartels will continue to profit. Today, these evil organizations—the Sinaloa Cartel, the Jalisco New Generation Cartel, and others—are switching their business models to take advantage of the weakness of our president. They have realized that there's more money to be made in smuggling children over our border than drugs.

Kids over kilos, as I once put it in one of my scripts.

According to a recent analysis by the *New York Post*, some cartels have even begun offering "VIP packages" worth more than $15,000 to people looking to sneak into the country. For years, these cartels have been building underground tunnels to smuggle cocaine, heroin, and fentanyl into the country; now, they don't need to deal with the drugs, which is very difficult. They can just drive, walk, or ferry men, women, and children into the country, knowing that if they get caught, they'll pay no price for what they've done. In fact, under the current administration, the people who've been smuggled in by the cartels will be welcomed with open arms.

Keep in mind that these are some of the most brutal regimes on the planet. When a cartel member catches one of his rivals out in public, he drives that person out into the deserts of Mexico, ties him to a pole, and lights him on fire to burn alive. People who cross the cartels are often murdered and then hung from bridges as a warning to anyone else thinking about crossing them in the future.

---

4   David Leonhardt, "The Hard Truth about Immigration," *The Atlantic*, October 23, 2023, https://www.theatlantic.com/ideas/archive/2023/10/us-immigration-policy-1965-act/675724/ (accessed September 18, 2024).

It truly is important to understand the political landscape of Mexico. Corporate media celebrated the June 2024 election of Claudia Sheinbaum, the first woman ever to be president of the country. What they didn't mention is that the woman is a left-wing academic with strong ties to the current Marxist president, or that she rose to prominence while hundreds—and I mean hundreds—of politicians, political candidates, journalists, and other agents of change were being assassinated by cartels in Mexico. To this day, cartels are killing anyone who threatens the status quo. They effectively run all of Mexico. The state police work for them, and so does the government. This is simple logic. An agent of change of any kind is a threat to business for the Mexican cartels. With that line of reasoning, anyone who survives is, by definition, a friend, not an enemy.

The cartels are not just criminal organizations. They are a business enterprise, and right now, business is booming. Human trafficking, drug smuggling, and facilitating human trafficking. The cartels are making it clear: No one is safe. And the new president of Mexico is nothing more than a lackey for these cartels, sending innumerable people over the border every day.

To paraphrase a great man: When the cartels send their people, they're not sending their best.

They're bringing drugs.

They're bringing crime.

They're rapists.

Back in 2015, when Donald Trump said these words in the lobby of Trump Tower, he was lambasted as a monstrous racist by the legacy media. Major news organizations compared him to white supremacists for daring to speak the truth.

Today, as the horrific incidents pile up and we continue to pay the price for Democrat incompetence with American blood, it looks like President Trump might have been a little too kind in his assessment of our situation at the border. Thanks to Biden and Harris's open borders, a violent prison gang from Venezuela called Tren de Aragua has begun infiltrating the United States. The gang participates in all kinds of crimes, ranging from human trafficking to kidnapping to extortion, money laundering, and illicit drug trafficking. Many officials call the gang "MS-13 on steroids." In 2024, a full week before the government broke the story about this horrible gang, I was joined by Joseph Humire and Mark Morgan to discuss the gang's activities.

"First of all," said Humire, "Tren de Aragua is the fastest growing criminal organization in the world. Only seven years ago, they had a presence in just two countries: Venezuela and Colombia. Fast forward seven years and they're now present in ten countries throughout the entire hemisphere including multiple cities here in the United States. But before they terrorized major American cities here in the United States, they were terrorizing many major cities all throughout South America. In Chile, they killed cops. In Peru, they did human trafficking rings at nightclubs. In Colombia, they trafficked all kinds of migrants through the Darien Gap into Panama. This is a gang that specializes in the suffering of human people, whether it's trafficking them, smuggling them, or just straight extorting them inside their communities."

And now, thanks to Biden and Harris, they're right here in the United States.

On February 22, 2024, Laken Riley, a twenty-two-year-old nursing student at Augusta University, was brutally murdered while jogging on the University of Georgia campus in Athens, Georgia. Her attacker, Jose Ibarra, a Venezuelan national who had entered the United States illegally in 2022, was arrested shortly after the crime. Ibarra, who has been linked to the notorious Venezuelan gang Tren de Aragua, is accused of disfiguring Riley's skull during the attack, dragging her body to a secluded area, and preventing her from calling for help.

Anyone who thinks these people don't bring drugs, crime, and dramatically increased rates of sexual assault simply isn't paying attention.

Or maybe they were on a long vacation during the horrible seven-day stretch between June 16 and June 22, 2024—a week that clearly illustrates why we need to secure our borders immediately. As you read this, please keep in mind that everything you're about to read happened over the course of *one week*. In the United States of America, once one of the safest and most prosperous nations in the world. I covered every second of it on Newsmax.

And none of it should have been allowed to happen in the first place.

～

It began on June 16.

That evening, police in Tulsa, Oklahoma, entered a bar and arrested a thin, scraggly man named Victor Martinez Hernandez. Ten months earlier, Hernandez had allegedly cornered Rachel Morin, a mother of five, while she was hiking alone on a trail in Baltimore, Maryland, beating her and raping her before leaving her to die.

During the relentless ten-month manhunt that followed, Hernandez slithered into the shadows, hiding out with family in Baltimore. It was all too easy for him to evade capture— after all, he was a ghost in the system, having slipped into the country illegally from El Salvador, where he was already a fugitive for a heinous murder. But Hernandez's trail of terror didn't stop there. Just days after his arrest, officials uncovered the horrifying truth: This monster had also savagely attacked a nine-year-old girl during a vicious home invasion in Los

Angeles in March 2023. The DNA evidence from this despicable crime is what finally brought him to justice in Tulsa.

One day later, on June 17, a machete-wielding illegal alien from Ecuador was charged with raping a thirteen-year-old girl in a New York City park in broad daylight. Much like Victor Martinez Hernandez, Christian Geovanny Inga-Landi, a twenty-five-year-old, came illegally into the country through Eagle Pass, Texas. He was released into the interior of the country and given a court date. When he failed to show up for that court date in February 2022, a federal immigration judge ordered him deported.

But he was already walking around in the middle of the country, likely looking for someone else to murder in cold blood.

That very same summer day, police in Houston, Texas, came upon the body of a twelve-year-old girl named Jocelyn Nungaray in a creek. It didn't take long to figure out that two illegal aliens named Johan Jose Martinez-Rangel and Franklin Pena were responsible. They had crossed the border three months earlier. One of them told Border Patrol that he was afraid he would be killed if he returned to his home country, an extremely common tactic of illegal border crossers. Although it's absolutely disgusting, this works. Once someone says "asylum," or that they're afraid for their lives, we allow them to stay, never considering the safety of American citizens who are defenseless against this kind of crime and depravity.

I can only imagine the fear that little Jocelyn, who'd been followed by the two thugs as she left a convenience store near her house, felt when she spotted them behind her. So, spare me the sob stories and the lies about amnesty. Right now, there is a mother who has lost the most important person in the world to her, and she's never going to get her back. All because one political party in this country thinks it's inconvenient to talk about the situation at our border.

In the aftermath of Jocelyn's murder, her mother spoke to the local outlet KHOU, speaking directly to the person who'd killed her child.

"She was so young," she said. "You took my baby away. You took her away. Now I get to let her little brother know his older sister is never coming home."

One day after *that*, on June 18, a man named Sakir Akkan was arrested in Albany, where police say he had allegedly raped a fifteen-year-old girl in his car after threatening to beat her with a pipe. By now, I'm sure I don't have to tell you that Akkan, like all the despicable lowlifes we've covered in this section so far, was an illegal immigrant who never should have been in this country in the first place.

These criminals are lowlifes who deserve the maximum punishment. And what makes it all so outrageous is that these illegals shouldn't have even been here.

In late June, I had the honor of interviewing Agnes Gibboney, an "angel mom" whose son Ronald da Silva was killed by an illegal immigrant. She told me, "My son was the best child any mother could ever ask to have. My son died saving his friend for whom the bullet was intended. I didn't find that out until twenty years later, when the intended target passed away and she told me that my son gave her son twenty years of life. That's the kind of person my son was.... Most of all, I miss all his hugs and his love, and I've been without my son for the past twenty-two years, and in twenty-two years, Bianca, nothing has improved in our country as far as securing our border. The guy that murdered my son was a known gang member who got arrested, was supposed to be deported, and the judge let him go."

I asked Agnes if she had a message for the parents of Jocelyn Nungaray. She shook her head solemnly and said: "First of all, I want to tell the families I am so sorry. I know what your life is going to be because now you too will have a life sentence of grief and pain. It is not fair, but what I would like to tell the parents is: Reach out to other mothers who have gone through this experience for moral support, because it is important to have that moral support.... Reach out. Don't despair. Their daughter will live forever in their hearts and in the hearts of others, and people like me, the angel moms like me, will always honor and respect your loved one, unlike this president."

Shortly after this wave of high-profile incidents in 2024, many people spoke out. One of them was the former lieutenant governor of New York, Betsy McCaughey, who hosts a show on Newsmax 2. In an op-ed for the *New York Post*, she wrote that Joe Biden's failure to secure our border had led to a plague of "femicide" across the United States.

While this carnage was going on, President Biden was at Camp David, spending seven full days preparing for his first debate with President Trump. He could not even find it in his heart to express sympathy for these families. And considering how that debate went for Joe, who knows *what* he was doing up at Camp David. As Seb Gorka quipped to me during an interview with *Newsline* in the lead-up to the debate, "They have two talking points: January 6 and abortion. It takes seven days to memorize that?"

Apparently, it took a long time, because President Biden didn't bother to comment on the death of these American citizens—the people he'd sworn to protect when he took the oath of office in January 2021—until days later. I'm sure that he didn't want to comment because deep down in whatever regions of his brain were still operational, he might have remembered that he allowed this crisis to happen on *day one* of his administration to fulfill his campaign promise to open our borders. This was planned, and it was executed exactly as the radical Left dreamed it would be. Progressives have been advertising their open-border policies for years, promising free stuff and amnesty. It's no wonder so many people showed up.

Even days later, commenting on the death of Rachel Morin, the mother of five who'd been killed on the trail in Baltimore, this was the best Biden could do: "We extend our deepest condolences to the family and loved ones of Rachel Morin. We cannot comment on active law enforcement cases. But fundamentally, we believe that people should be held accountable to the fullest extent of the law if they are found to be guilty."

When you've worked in journalism for a few years (or almost three decades, as I have), you get used to the language of press releases and public statements that have been reviewed by ten lawyers. *That* is all this statement was. Joe Biden couldn't have spoken from his shriveled black raisin of a heart to these families if his life depended on it. To him, the deaths of these young women was nothing more than a political inconvenience. In his mind, they did nothing more than remind people of all the steps he'd taken to *help* illegal immigrants get into this country, all because he'd promised to do just that on the campaign trail.

Another clue that the statement was nothing more than a pre-written brush-off from the Biden White House? They sent the *same one* about Jocelyn Nungaray. Like, *exactly* the same one. I put them side by side on the screen during my *Newsline* broadcast to show that they were almost verbatim. Only the name and a few words in the opening line were changed.

"Our hearts go out to the family and loved ones of Jocelyn Nungaray. We cannot comment on active law enforcement cases," the statement continued. "But fundamentally, anyone found guilty of this type of heinous and shocking crime should be held accountable, to the fullest extent of the law."

When it comes to lyrical defenses of the rights of drag queens, the Biden White House seems willing to spend hours crafting prose—really sweating over whether this or that current event represents "an unprecedented assault on LGBTQ+ rights" or "the worst assault on LGBTQ+ rights in history." The same goes for Joe Biden's statements in support of his crackhead criminal son, Hunter. But the families of innocent American citizens who've effectively been murdered by the Biden-Harris administration's dereliction of duty get a form letter and the White House's "deepest condolences."

This is both heartbreaking and enraging.

President Trump, in sharp contrast, understood the dangers posed by illegal immigration from day one. He was willing to tell the truth when no other politicians would. And unlike most politicians, he was able and willing to fight off the smears that came from the media, who seemed to believe anyone who didn't want to allow murderers and rapists into this country was a racist. President Trump had also seen a great deal of suffering during his presidency. And unlike Joe Biden, he never turned away from it. And yet CNN has the nerve to call Joe Biden "the Empathizer in Chief," writing long articles about his ability to connect with people about grief.

Please.

The *only* one speaking to these families about what they've gone through is Donald Trump, who never seeks acclaim for his kindness. That's why, rather than hiding from the issue, he called the family of Rachel Morin, expressed real condolences for their suffering, and invited them to be his personal guests at his rally in late June. He also invited the family of one of the victims to lunch. There, I'm sure it was comforting for Rachel Morin's mother to be surrounded by people who weren't afraid to say her daughter's name—who didn't want to sweep the whole thing under the rug because it was politically inconvenient. When President Trump said Rachel Morin's name onstage in Pennsylvania, the crowd erupted in applause. They began chanting "Build the Wall!"

I'm sure it didn't even come close to taking away the unimaginable pain of losing a child. I know that, sometimes, it can help grieving family members to know that the loss of their loved ones will not be in vain—that some good, however small, might come from the loss they've suffered. If nothing else, it can be comforting for a grieving mother and father to know that because of what they've had to endure, the chances of it ever happening to someone else might decrease by just a little.

If nothing else, the cheers at the rally were better than silence, which is what Rachel Morin's family got from the United States government. Just days earlier, Secretary Alejandro Mayorkas—the man charged with keeping our borders secure—had failed to say Rachel Morin's name on CNN. Instead, he'd simply repeated the White House's pre-approved language on the matter, saying, "Of course, our hearts break for the children, the families, the loved ones, the friends, of the individual who was murdered, the woman, the mother."[5]

Again, this is the kind of language that's supposed to cloud your senses and make your eyes glaze over.

Don't let it.

Say their names.

Rachel Morin was a mother of five children. She was a daughter. She was about to be a grandmother. Speaking on television later that evening, Rachel's mother said that Mayorkas's words "totally depersonalized her daughter and made her an object." She said, "To not even acknowledge that my daughter is a person or that she's a female or that she's a

---

5   Maria Lencki, "Mother of Rachel Morin: The Biden administration doesn't 'value life,'" Fox News, June 22, 2024, https://www.foxnews.com/media/mother-rachel-morin-biden-administration-doesnt-value-life (accessed Sep-tember 7, 2024).

mother...to categorize her as a statistic...it just shows how impersonal they are. How they don't value life."[6]

Another vile example, in June 2024, is when Joy Reid was interviewing Congresswoman Pramila Jayapal of Washington state, and mocked conservative outlets for covering the rape of a little girl, allegedly at the hands of an illegal. Reid called it "fearmongering." To gaslight, she threw up screenshots of three major cable networks: CNN, MSNBC, and Fox News.

"Look," she said. "Here's the three cable networks. Our banner said 'Biden announces new protections for some undocumented spouses.' CNN says, 'Biden announces protections for some undocumented spouses.' Here was Fox's banner: 'Migrant arrested for raping thirteen-year-old girl.'"

In response, Congresswoman Jayapal laughed and said, "Yes! That's part of the problem."

"Part of the problem," said Joy Reid.

Now, I don't know what has to be wrong with a person's brain that lets them giggle about the rape of a thirte-year-old girl, and I hope I never have to find out. Every night, Joy Reid goes on television and works herself up to the point of hysteria about racism, white supremacy, and the imaginary threat of "fascism" from the right. But when it comes to the brutal rape of a thirteen-year-old: She laughs.

Let's not forget that this is the same Joy Reid who, in her old blog posts, speculated mockingly about then Florida Governor Charlie Crist's sexuality, referring to him as "Miss Charlie," and stated that "most straight people cringe at the sight of two men kissing." Reid also made inflammatory comments about the 9/11 attacks, promoting conspiracy theories that suggested they were an inside job. It's appalling that she dismissed these hurtful and baseless claims as hacking attempts on her blog. Yeah, (eye roll) sure you were hacked!

---

6   Ibid.

As the clip of Joy Reid giggling made its way around the internet, we were reminded of another MSNBC clip—this one featuring former White House Press Secretary Jen Psaki, host Rachel Maddow, and a few others (including Joy Reid) doing a roundtable the night of Super Tuesday 2024. In this clip, Psaki expresses confusion about why voters in her home state of Virginia were so concerned about immigration when the border is thousands of miles away.

At this point, Rachel Maddow jumps in from her perch in her ivory tower and says, "Well, Virginia does share a border with *West* Virginia. Very contested area."[7]

Get it?

Most people from West Virginia are white, so according to the rules of woke media, you're allowed to dehumanize and mock them all you want. The fact that *those* people are poor and suffering—largely due to the closure of coal mines that were once the lifeblood of the state—is funny to Democrats and media elites. In the clip, shrill cackling erupts from every member of the panel. Jen Psaki might live in Virginia, but she definitely does *not* live in the real world. If she did, she would have known why Ted Cruz demanded an apology from her the next day. The Texas senator revealed that a two-year-old who was on a walk with his mother was shot and killed, reportedly by an El Salvadoran illegal immigrant, just a thirty-minute drive from Psaki's $1.7 million mansion. When innocents are being murdered, illegal immigration is not a laughing matter.

Once again, if these MSNBC talking heads bothered to get out and talk to people—which is what journalists are supposed to do—they might have a better idea of what voters care about. If they ever left their expensive apartments and

---

7   John Lynch, "West Virginia 'mocked' on MSNBC by Jen Psaki and Rachel Maddow," WTRF, March 6, 2024, https://www.wtrf.com/west-virginia/west-virginia-mocked-on-msnbc-by-jen-psaki-and-rachel-maddow/ (accessed September 7, 2024).

well-appointed studios, maybe it wouldn't come as such a surprise that millions of people all over this country think they're
braindead morons. I'd invite any one of them to get on a plane
(first class, if they want) and travel with me to the crossing
points in Arizona, California, and Texas, just to see what
the people in these towns go through. I'd like them to speak
with the ranchers who live just a few miles from the border,
who are often forced to defend their own homes with shot-
guns from bloodthirsty members of Mexican cartels. I'd like
them to watch as hundreds of children a day come streaming
across border crossings faster than the men and women of law
enforcement can catch them, disappearing with human traffickers into the United States, never to be heard from again.

Maybe then, the fact that eighty-five thousand migrant
children have gone missing under the care of Joe Biden and
Alejandro Mayorkas might sink in. This isn't just a failure;
it's an abomination. It's mind-boggling that we're supposed to
just accept that tens of thousands of children have vanished,
falling into the hands of predators and traffickers while this
administration stands by, apparently too busy or too indif-
ferent to care. This is the horrific reality that Biden's policies
have unleashed.

Over the years, I've found that seeing things up close is the
only way to truly understand what's going on. Whenever possible, I try to speak with people who've been directly involved
in events, getting their impressions while things are still fresh.

And that's why I've returned to the border so many times
as a journalist.

You can't believe it until you see it with your own eyes.

The first time I saw the southern border in person, it was the
late 1990s. I had just moved to San Diego from Albany taking
a reporter job at KGTV, the local ABC affiliate. The border

was effectively our backyard, and there were endless stories to investigate and report on. Now, instead of covering blizzards and political backroom horse trading, I found myself reporting on wildfires and the pandas at the San Diego Zoo.

But my biggest investigative stories all involved the southern border, less than an hour's drive from my home in La Jolla. Back then, illegal crossings were a fraction of the stampedes we've experienced recently, but there was more than enough to keep a young reporter busy.

Fortunately, I had an amazing cameraman named Guillermo who could chat up locals and help us get the inside scoop at the border. Memo (his Spanish nickname) and I worked the night shift together for months, driving across the border in the station's navy blue Jeep Cherokee covering the many weird stories that were constant. One night, we met up with coyote, a human smuggler, who gave me precise details of how he trafficked people across the border.

Some days, I went out with Border Patrol agents in vans, watching them comb the sand for footprints left by migrants. In those days, officers would literally get down on their hands and knees, trying to trace the path that incoming migrants had taken. This old-school technique, known as "sign cutting," involves looking for water splashes and footprints in the dirt, just like you see in the old movies. According to my sources, it remains one of the most effective methods for tracking people who don't want to be found. Some nights, I would sit up all night in the car on a stakeout, just waiting to catch a glimpse of someone crossing the border, wanting to get their stories and find out what had made them risk the dangerous journey north. One night, I got lucky and saw two people.

Two.

It's amazing to look back on how quaint things used to be.

Once, I got a tip that there was a factory in San Diego that hired illegal workers and locked them in overnight. My source told me about a place where I could see groups of illegal immigrants jump into the vans that would pick them up here in the United States just after they came across the border. Another photographer named Rhett and I went to San Ysidro, just north of the Tijuana crossing, and waited. Sure enough, a bunch of illegals hopped into the van and headed right to the factory. Hours later, like clockwork, the doors closed. No one was leaving that night. We did surveillance for a few days, capturing footage of illegals coming and going as the factory swapped out its illegal workers.

We had the story and now wanted to get a comment from the factory owner. When I confronted him, he ran away and hid from Rhett's camera.

No surprise there.

When the piece aired on my station, KGTV, it got the attention of the feds, and because of my story, they were able to make their case. As a result, my crew and I were invited to be there when they raided the factory. Naturally, we had cameras rolling. The factory owner was not happy to see them either, especially since they shut down the operation. My team and I would win a San Diego press club investigative award for the story. Exposing that sweatshop showed the depravity that is often visited upon illegals. So often, they are taken advantage of and put in dangerous conditions, and unfortunately many of them are women and children.

Often, we would be chasing news in Tijuana, a rough city and the busiest border crossing in the world (and also, oddly enough, the birthplace of the Caesar salad). It's a place a twenty-two-year-old woman doesn't go and hang around without a good sidekick. On one particularly slow news day, we were feeling ambitious and decided to approach a group of men who we knew were coyotes. One of them was willing to tell me about his life's work, but he wasn't willing to show me his face. So, Guillermo and I came up with an idea. I would interview the man as usual, but Guillermo would aim his camera at the ground, where our silhouettes were clearly visible thanks to the hot afternoon sun overhead. The resulting image was chilling: a dark silhouette of a man, speaking about the dark deeds he had committed ferrying people into the United States in secret. In that interview, as well as a few others I conducted during my time in San Diego, I learned that the job of the coyote is often passed down through families over generations.

These interviews were chilling. So were the dozens of stories I did about illegal immigration in the late 1990s and early 2000s. In those days, it was still common to hear Republicans *and* Democrats discuss the need to secure our border with some kind of fence or barrier. In 1996, the section on immigration from the Democratic Party's platform read:

> Today's Democratic Party...believes we must remain a nation of laws. We cannot tolerate illegal immigration and we must stop it. For years before Bill Clinton became president, Washington talked tough but failed to act. In 1992, our borders might as well not have existed. The border was under-patrolled, and what patrols there were, were under-equipped. Drugs flowed freely. Illegal immigration was rampant. Criminal immigrants, deported after committing crimes in America, returned the very next day to commit crimes again.[8]

In other words: *They're bringing drugs. They're bringing crime.* Huh.

---

8   Matt Welch, "Democrats on Immigration Since 1980: From Apathy to Anger to Amnesty (of Sorts)," *Reason*, August 27, 2015, https://reason. com/2015/08/27/democrats-on-immigration-since-1980-from/ (accessed September 7, 2024).

Now where have I heard *that* before?

Back in the '90s, when I covered stories about illegal immigration, it wasn't the left-right issue that it is today. Everyone seemed to agree that allowing people to come into this country from Mexico, where drugs and crime *were* rampant, was a bad idea. The platform "more is better, less is racist" didn't exist in the Democratic Party. In 2006, when I was covering local news in Boston, Democrats even voted to put up additional border fencing. Even then, everyone seemed to understand the importance of having a border. Without one, the United States would cease to be a sovereign nation.

This changed over the years as Democrats, now led by Barack Obama, began to believe that if they gave illegal immigrants citizenship, they'd vote Democrat forever. Over time, any talk of border security or enforcing our laws disappeared from the immigration section of the Democratic Party's platform. Instead, we got language about inclusivity and the rights of all the people who'd come here illegally. We began to hear phrases like "no human being is illegal," and long speeches about how this country should welcome everyone—even those who break the law—in with open arms. It didn't matter if these people were violent criminals, or if they posed a danger to people in the United States. Last year, Border Patrol encountered a staggering 172 people on the FBI's terror watch list at the border. And again, that doesn't include the ones who managed to evade capture.

Those people are in this country right now, and we have no idea where they are or what they're planning.

During the Trump presidency, as the administration worked to stem the tide of illegals flowing across the border, the corporate media and the radical Left worked against the White House every step of the way. Jim Acosta of CNN stood up every few weeks in the briefing room to recite poetry about the United States being "a nation of immigrants." Democrats in Congress abruptly switched positions on the need for a wall at our border, pretending that there was, in fact, no problem with illegal immigration. The problems with drugs, crime, and human trafficking disappeared from the corporate media's coverage. The Biden-Harris administration wanted to deny that they had created an invasion. I knew the leftist media was lying for them.

It was August 2021, and I decided I needed to go back to the border and bring the American people the truth. I wasn't affiliated with a network at the time, so I went as a freelancer and paid my own way, just to see what I could find. A few months earlier, I'd gotten word that there were huge numbers of people crossing the border in Del Rio, a section of Texas that had long been a hotbed for illegal crossings. I flew to Dallas and met up with my cousin, who has always been game for a road trip, especially one with no set itinerary or return date. It's no surprise, since we de la Garzas come from a line of conquistadors. In fact, there is a statue of one of my ancestors Blas Maria Falcon de la Garza in Corpus Christi, Texas. He colonized that part of Texas and the border of Mexico, later bringing over the longhorns that were instrumental in ranching. My cousin and I rented a car and headed south, down to the land where my ancestors once walked. As I drove, I knew this border would be dramatically different from the one I had covered decades earlier. I didn't know what I was going to find there. I didn't know which town we'd end up in, or where we would sleep once we got there. I only knew that I needed to see what was really going on. Sitting at home and getting my news from other sources—even when those sources were trustworthy—wasn't enough for me. As usual, I had to see it with my own eyes.

Once we arrived in McAllen, Texas, I placed a few calls to my sources in law enforcement and chatted up a few local reporters who were at the bus station doing live reports. Over the years, I've found that it's usually local reporters who can give you the best tips about a city. They know where all the action is. From these conversations, I learned that there was an outdoor migrant detention camp under a bridge nearby, and that a few networks had been allowed in to film and interview people. But by the time I arrived, they'd kicked all media outlets out of the area. I needed to improvise.

During my first days in town, I'd heard about a pastor who would often go to the border and pray with migrants as they came over. Locals called him "the pistol-packing pastor," because he never went to the border without a gun in his waistband. I managed to track down his wife on Facebook, and before I knew it, I was in the back of a van with the pistol-packing pastor himself, his wife, and a few volunteers from their church, headed toward the border to get the lay of the land. In the van, there were protein bars and bottles of water. The pastor told me that he'd once seen a baby come across the border with a note stuffed into his diaper with an address.

Please take me to this family, the note said.

When we arrived, I saw the National Guard from Texas, which was there simply to keep the peace, not to make arrests. Border Patrol had set up plastic folding tables that would serve as processing centers. It was a neighborhood street, and my new pastor pal drove a bit farther. Off the paved roads, the dirt trails led close to the border. It was about eleven o'clock at night. Figures approached in the distance.

"Look," said someone behind me. "There's a group coming now."

Up ahead, a mass of at least three hundred illegals appeared on the horizon, walking slowly toward a small group of agents who would line them up and then take them back up the hill to the makeshift processing tables with bags and belongings in their hands. Four or five Border Patrol agents walked in front of them, leading the way. I watched, stunned, as the people lined up, gave their names to the people at the tables and then they were ushered into buses to be taken to a holding area for the night.

I walked down to the Rio Grande river and approached them as they got off the makeshift rafts. Very few spoke English. One of the ones who did was a child. When I asked her and her parents why they made the journey up from Venezuela, they all said the same thing.

"Joe Biden."

Months earlier, Joe Biden had won the presidency by promising to do exactly the opposite of everything President Trump had done, including opening the border wide to anyone who desired to come. Around this time, I'd seen reports of thousands of people crossing the border in Biden-Harris 2020 T-shirts. The illegals I interviewed on this night in August 2021 were no different. Although they didn't wear campaign swag, they had come because they'd gotten the message that Joe Biden and the Democrats had been sending for the entirety of the 2020 campaign season: The border is wide open again; if you can get here, you'll be able to stay.

That night, the pastor and his wife prayed with the migrants. People cried and thanked Jesus that they'd made the journey alive. For six days, they'd been traveling with smugglers, not knowing whether they would ever arrive, or what this strange new land would be like when they got here. The Border Patrol separated the men from the women but allowed families to stay together. All their belongings—IDs, cell phones, and wallets—went into plastic bags. As the people were processed at the plastic tables, I asked the pastor how things had changed since the Biden-Harris administration began.

He said there was more crime, and that migrants were crossing in broad daylight, and some were breaking into homes. He told me that the children were not safe.

To this day, I consider the pastor and his wife good friends, though we don't speak as often as I'd like. To be clear, neither of them support illegal immigration, but, as pastors, they are called to be the hands and feet of God. For them, being on the front lines to offer a prayer and some cold water when people first step foot on US soil is what, as Christians, Jesus has called them to do. They are a beautiful couple.

After my experience with them, when I left that night at 3 a.m., not only did I have the footage, but I had a deeper understanding of the reality at the border. But I knew, because of Biden's irresponsible actions, that things were going to get worse. The Border Patrol facilities I'd seen simply didn't have the capacity to handle hundreds of people marching across the border every day—especially since Joe Biden had destroyed everything that President Trump had done to keep this country safe.

Several executive orders signed during Biden's first hundred days in office severely rolled back border protections. He signed a "Proclamation on Ending Discriminatory Bans on Entry to the United States." He signed a "Proclamation on the Termination of Emergency with Respect to the Southern Border of the United States and Redirection of Funds Diverted to Border Wall Construction," and many others, which can all be found on the White House's website (because remember, these people are *proud* of these executive orders; they don't feel any shame about the horror they've unleashed on towns and cities all over this country).

Whenever I report a story about migrant caravans heading for the southern border of the United States—which I do with shocking regularity these days—I think of what it was like to stand on the border in Texas and see that mass of people coming at me. That night, the three hundred or so people who crossed the border looked mostly harmless; as far as I could tell, the group didn't contain any rapists, murderers, or people secretly ferrying drugs from Mexico. But that's the problem. You usually can't tell until it's too late.

But Joe Biden doesn't care. Neither does Kamala Harris, who was the border czar under Joe Biden, no matter what the corporate press says about it. They want this to happen. In March 2024, a federal judge ruled that the Biden administration's program to allow thirty thousand migrants into the country *per month* could not be challenged in court by the attorney general of Texas. The lawsuit was dismissed, and as of this writing in the summer of 2024, the migrants continue to stream across the border. This, as Senator J.D. Vance told me during my exclusive interview with him at the border, is all about getting new voters for the Democrats.

Shortly after the ruling, I spoke with Kari Lake, the former news anchor and gubernatorial candidate who'd just announced a run for the US Senate in Arizona. Unlike Joe Biden, Kamala Harris, and most Democrats, Kari Lake is a person who's seen the border up close. During her campaign for governor in 2020, she released a playbook that border states could use to secure their borders even in the face of opposition from the federal government.

"The states can take control of the border because the U.S. Constitution allows them to do that under Article One, Section Ten, Clause Three. When the federal government fails to protect us in the event of an invasion, the states can take over. And that's what we're starting to see in Texas. And boy! The federal government is fighting back like a child throwing a temper tantrum, and I'm glad that Greg Abbott is not backing down. The states absolutely have the right, and the duty to do this, and they should get busy right away."

In the spring of 2024 seeing that immigration was a huge issue for the American people, Joe Biden signed an executive order that was designed to make it *look* like he was addressing the situation at the border. But it was too little, too late.

Millions of people had already streamed across the border, disappearing into towns and cities all over the country. Among them were the suspects charged with killing Jocelyn Nungaray, Rachel Morin, and Laken Riley in cold blood. The names of these victims will go down in history beside the names of Aiden Clark, Christopher Gadd, Travis Wolfe, and Kate Steinle, all of whom were killed by illegal immigrants who never should have been in this country in the first place. Tragically, we probably haven't seen the end of the carnage that will occur as a result of the Biden-Harris administration's severe dereliction of duty on this issue. President Biden should have been impeached over this. Of course, given the way the Mayorkas impeachment went, it probably wouldn't have passed. Crime will continue to rise as every American town becomes a border town. More innocent Americans will lose their lives. According to several experts I've spoken with over the past few months, a terrorist attack is not out of the question.

In the summer of 2024, eight men from Tajikistan with ties to the Islamic State were arrested after they crossed the southern border illegally. In March, a man from Lebanon who claimed to be a bomb maker working for the terror group Hezbollah was stopped near El Paso, Texas. An interrogation revealed that he was on his way to New York City, where he planned to "try to make a bomb." In March 2024, a Chinese national illegally entered the Marine Corps Air Ground Combat Center at Twentynine Palms, California, before being detained by military law enforcement. This incident is part of a broader trend, with Chinese nationals reportedly gaining unauthorized access to US military bases and sensitive sites nearly a hundred times in recent years.

As you read these stories, bear in mind that since 2021, more than 1.8 million people have been classified as "gotaways" by Border Patrol, a number that doesn't even include the people who've managed to slip by completely undetected. As Sheriff Chad Bianco of Riverside County, California, told me in June 2024 on *Newsline*, "The president and the president's administration think that the rest of the country is stupid. They think we can't look out our front door and our back door and see what's going on at the border. The cartels 100 percent control our border. Our government knows it, and they don't care."

As Sheriff Bianco spoke, soundless videos of men, women, and children crossing the border played on the screen. As they did, he pointed out that these images of women and children didn't quite capture the current reality of the border as he saw it.

"Those [crossings] happen once in a while," he explained. "Ninety percent of the people coming across the border are single males. We know they're criminals; we know they're coming into this country to do us harm. The FBI admits that they are here to do us harm. They have no idea how many, or where they are, or what they're planning. This is a powder keg waiting to explode, and the president is the cause. He could have stopped this anytime. Instead, he purposely caused it his first day in office, and this right now is a ploy for votes, and it is disgusting that our government is so dysfunctional for the destruction of our country."

Sheriff Bianco was right in more ways than one. If the Democrats get their way, illegal immigrants will soon be able to damage this country in yet another serious way: by voting in our elections. Recently, it's been revealed that welfare offices all over the country have been handing out voter registration forms (and, in some cases, mail-in ballots), to people without requiring proof of citizenship. The only state where this *doesn't* occur is Arizona, where Republicans passed a law making it illegal. Everywhere else, including at the federal level, the practice remains completely legal.

It makes perfect sense. Democrats allow millions of people to walk into this country—so many, in fact, that we couldn't possibly keep track of them all—and then hands out voter registration forms to them without requiring proof of citizenship. They do this assuming that the people will be so grateful that they'll vote Democrat for their rest of their lives. As far as Democrats are concerned, anyone with brown skin or Hispanic heritage is going to vote for Kamala Harris no matter what. How couldn't they, given how hard Donald Trump has been on illegal immigration?

Luckily, they're wrong about that. During President Trump's four years in office, his support among Hispanic voters surged. The same thing is true of his support among *all* minority groups, despite the legacy media's constant attempts to portray him as a racist (with no evidence whatsoever). Recently, it's been reported that Trump and his new administration plan to conduct a record number of deportations during his second term. Legacy media institutions are pulling their hair out when they have to report on this.

But Hispanic voters—this one in particular—think it's great. We know better than anyone what it's like to come to the United States legally, following all the laws and waiting in all the lines necessary to become a citizen. When my father's family did it in the early twentieth century, they had to work their butts off. By the time my grandparents had gone through the process, they knew more about this country than most. New citizens who go through legal pathways need to know, among other things, the intricacies of our three branches of government as well as a great deal of information about our founding fathers. When they stand up at their naturalization ceremonies and recite the pledge of allegiance, they do so as Americans in every sense of the word.

The people who simply break the law and walk across the border are different. These people, the vast majority of whom are single men, don't want to work to become citizens. They want to collect all the free stuff that the Biden administration has been all too willing to provide. Free phones, debit cards, and thousands of dollars a month for provisions, not to mention free stays in fancy hotels—all while Americans go hungry and struggle. All that the Democrats ask for in exchange, it seems, are votes. The Republicans in Congress passed the SAVE (Safeguard American Voter Eligibility) Act to curtail the horrible practice of non-citizen voting, but the Senate Democrats refused to take it up.

In August 2024, I had the honor of traveling to the border with Senator Vance, who had just been named Donald Trump's 2024 running mate. My day began early, roused by my iPhone alarm at 5 a.m., in Sierra Vista, Arizona. The sun had barely risen as I prepared for an exclusive sit-down with Senator Vance at Montezuma Pass, a notorious stretch of the border where cell service is nonexistent, and the wall abruptly stops.

This wasn't my first time at Montezuma Pass. Back in the 1990s, during my San Diego reporting days, I had spent hours staking out this very area, where we might spot one or two illegal crossers over a ten-hour shift. But as I arrived at the meeting point on August 1, 2024, it was clear that things had changed dramatically. The place was swarming with agents—not just for the cameras, but for security. The Border Patrol Tactical Unit (BORTAC), a special unit of the Border Patrol, was on high alert, and with good reason. Kamala Harris had once suggested in 2018 that Congress should eliminate Immigration and Customs Enforcement (ICE), saying, "we need to probably think about starting from scratch." God only knows what she would want to do with these brave men and women now.

Boy, was I glad they were there that day. As I was about to find out, Montezuma Pass had only grown more dangerous since my last visit. Just as we were about to roll, the sound of helicopters filled the air. Senator Vance, ever vigilant, pointed out a drone from the Mexican side flying overhead. He informed me that migrants were approaching, just two miles south of our location.

Later, I learned that those large construction trucks parked along the wall weren't just there for show either. According to a Border Patrol source, there was a high probability that armed individuals were on the other side of the wall, ready to cross. The source confided in me that he wouldn't have chosen this location for the interview due to the risks—especially in a post-assassination-attempt world. It's one thing to be surveilled by a drone, but the potential threat of gunmen nearby brought a whole new level of urgency to the situation.

"We're in our country," Senator Vance said, "the United States of America, and we're worried about drones invading our airspace when the vice-presidential nominee is here for an interview.... They say they want to import millions of illegal aliens, give them the right to vote, give them amnesty, and then they don't have to worry about persuading their own citizens anymore because they then have imported a new group of voters. And it's really scandalous if you think about, why wouldn't you want to persuade your own people that you have the best policies to improve their lives?"

Shortly after the interview, the *New York Times* reported that the Biden-Harris administration has begun naturalizing immigrants at a furious rate. In 2021, it took an average of 11.5 months to become a citizen; in the lead-up to the election—when Biden and Harris happened to want lots of new people to vote Democrat—it was taking just 4.9 months.

Of course, we know why Kamala Harris and Tim Walz want to stay away from the issues. It's because they've been disastrous for the American people, allowing rioting and a full-scale invasion of the country. I can only hope that when they lose in November 2024, they'll get the message loud and clear.

In the meantime, I'm planning to stay on the front lines of this crisis, bringing the truth about it to the American people. I'll continue to speak with the knowledgeable experts and contributors such as Mark Morgan, former Acting Secretary of Homeland Security Chad Wolf, and border correspondent Jason Jones, who know better than anyone what's going on at our southern border.

Who knows?

Maybe Alejandro Mayorkas will finally answer my calls and agree to come on *Newsline* to be interviewed.

But I'm not counting on it.

He's probably afraid I'll make a citizen's arrest right there in the studio!

CHAPTER SEVEN

THE "CHEAP FAKE" NEWS

Eight seconds.

That's about how long it took Democrats all over the United States to realize they were in deep trouble. As Joe Biden shuffled onto the debate stage on June 27, 2024, it was clear right away that the night wasn't going to go well. The man moved like a zombie who'd just crawled out of a grave; his face had the blank, faraway look of a deer in headlights. And he spoke like...

Well, I'm not even sure *what* to compare it to.

"Look," he said a few minutes in, responding in hushed tones to a question about abortion. "There's so many young women who have been...including a young woman who just was murdered and he went to the funeral. The idea that she was murdered by—by—by an immigrant coming in and ghskfi [*sic*] talk about that. But here's the deal, there's a lot of young women who are being raped by their...by their in-laws, by their...by their spouses, brothers and sisters, by...just...it's just...it's just ridiculous. And they can do nothing about it. And they try to arrest them when they cross state lines."

An *actual* deer in headlights probably could have performed better.

Over the course of about two hours, as Democrats all over the country recoiled from their televisions in horror, one thing became clear. The president of the United States was not up to the job of running for reelection, or of continuing to serve as president (not that he ever was in the first place). Biden's time on the stage featured several lapses just like the one quoted above, including a full minute of nonsense that ended with the phrase "We beat Medicare." His performance was nothing short of frightening, a total and complete display of his cognitive tailspin. The contrast with President Trump, who stood by quietly as Biden dug his own grave, could not have been clearer. Where Biden was rambling and incoherent, President Trump was sharp and cogent. No one who watched the full debate could deny that election night in November, if Biden remained on the ticket, was going to be a landslide.

And unlike 2020, the Biden campaign couldn't just shove their candidate in a dark basement and have him do easy events over Zoom. This was going to be a real campaign, and if the first debate was any indication, Biden was not up to the task. Earlier in the night, I had tuned in, genuinely wondering if Biden might be able to pull out a drugged-up, State-of-the-Union-style performance. After all, we hadn't seen him in days, and he had surprised us all before. For all I knew, he'd been up at Camp David getting worked on like the Russian fighter from *Rocky IV*, preparing to fool everyone into thinking he was competent for two hours.

But what the American people saw could not be unseen. Calls for Biden to drop out were finally voiced and taken seriously by the corporate press. Even Van Jones, Biden's biggest fan on CNN, voiced some serious concerns. The cover-up was over. Soon, Joe Biden's campaign would be over, too.

After this, the legacy media, which had spent the past five years or so pretending that Joe Biden was just fine, couldn't deny that the man was barely there. Speaking on MSNBC, Joy Reid said, "My phone never really stopped buzzing throughout [the debate]. And the universal reaction was somewhere approaching panic. The people who were texting with me who were very concerned about President Biden seeming extremely feeble, seeming extremely weak."[1]

Funny. I seem to remember these same outlets telling us that anyone who raised questions about Joe Biden's deteriorating mental capacity was simply "repeating right-wing talking points." When my colleague James Rosen attempted to raise the issue respectfully during a rare Biden press briefing in January 2022, the president told him that he had "no idea" why a majority of Democrats would question his cognitive fitness.

Any liberal reporter who stepped out of line and tried to report the truth about our empty husk of a president was shamed into silence by his or her colleagues. On June 4, a little less than a month before the debate, the *Wall Street Journal* published a long, deeply reported story titled "Behind Closed Doors, Biden Shows Signs of Slipping." The story included shocking details from dozens of White House aides and legislators who'd been in the room with the president, chronicling the rapid decline that had occurred over Biden's time in office.

The president, according to the story, had nodded off during meetings about Ukraine aid. He'd lost his train of thought repeatedly, and often had to resort to notes when speaking. The story also included several examples of Biden flubs that had occurred right out in public, where any reporter could have picked up on them.

For instance:

> On May 20, during a Rose Garden event celebrating Jewish American Heritage month, Biden

said one of the U.S. hostages held in Gaza was a guest at the White House event, before correcting himself. One day earlier, at a campaign event in Detroit, he indicated that he was vice president during the Covid-19 pandemic, which started three years after he left that office. It was one of numerous flubs in the single speech that prompted the White House to make corrections to the official transcript.

In January, he mixed up two of his Hispanic cabinet secretaries, Alejandro Mayorkas and Xavier Becerra. During a February fundraiser in New York, he recounted speaking to German Chancellor Helmut Kohl—who died in 2017— at the 2021 Group of Seven meeting. That same month, at a different fundraiser, he said that during the 2021 G-7 summit he had spoken to former French President François Mitterrand, who died in 1996.[2]

In response to the story, the legacy media went nuts. Joe Scarborough, host of *Morning Joe*, blasted the *Wall Street Journal* for publishing it in the first place. He also claimed, hilariously, that Joe Biden was sharper than ever.

"If you want to talk about international affairs," he said, "if you want to talk about how to get bipartisan legislation, Joe Biden is light-years ahead of all of them. And the fact that the *Wall Street Journal* knew these quotes were out there, that editors—I'm not talking about the reporter. People always

---

2   Annie Linskey and Siobhan Hughes, "Behind Closed Doors, Biden Shows Signs of Slipping," *The Wall Street Journal*, June 4, 2024, https://www.wsj.com/politics/policy/joe-biden-age-election-2024-8ee15246 (accessed September 8, 2024).

blame the reporter.... I don't even know what to say. I really don't even know what to say here."[3]

I'm not surprised. If *I* had spent the past five years gaslighting the country at the level Joe Scarborough has been doing it, I wouldn't know what to say either. Just two months before the *Wall Street Journal* published its story, Joe Scarborough had screamed at his viewers, saying that this addled version of Joe Biden was "the best Biden ever," and "f**k you if you don't believe it." He's such a charming guy, screaming at his audience and telling them what to think.

This is not the kind of thing you'd expect to hear from a free, independent press.

It's what you'd expect to hear from state-run TV in Russia or North Korea.

Which, sadly, is exactly what the corporate media in the United States has become. Rather than reporting accurately on the president of the United States, the "big three" networks—all of whom are owned by giant conglomerates with deep ties to the Democratic Party—have become the PR wing of the Biden White House. When Jen Psaki left her job as press secretary to become a commentator for MSNBC, her job description didn't change one bit. She, along with everyone else at CNN and the rest of the legacy media networks, made it their life's work to defend every move Joe Biden made.

When he mangled a sentence, they told us it was his stutter. When he forgot the names of world leaders, or called out to people in the audiences at his speeches who'd died decades ago, the supposedly "unbiased" pundits in the corporate press assured us that he was "intense" (Anderson Cooper), "lucid and well-informed" (Paul Krugman), and the victim

---

3   Brett Samuels, "White House fires back at Wall Street Journal over Biden story," *The Hill*, June 5, 2024, https://thehill.com/homenews/administration/4704853-white-house-wall-street-journal-biden/ (accessed September 8, 2024).

of "an age attack, this obsession by the right" (Ari Melber).[4] The White House press corps, which is supposed to be the American people's first line of defense against BS from whatever administration is in power, went right along with it. They ignored tips about the president being "completely checked out" during NATO meetings.[5] They refused to chase down stories about how much difficulty Biden was having staying awake past 4 p.m.

In the lead-up to the debate, as videos of Joe Biden nearly sleepwalking off stages spread around the internet like wildfire, these liberal pundits even latched onto a new term, "cheap fake," to discredit the footage. According to a story published in the *New York Times* on June 21, a "cheap fake" is a video of Joe Biden that has been "stripped of vital context to portray him in a negative light." Of course, the term didn't *really* enter the public lexicon until Press Secretary Karine Jean-Pierre trotted it out during a heated spat with my colleague James Rosen, who *again* raised the issue of Biden's age during a White House briefing—*two years* after he asked the first time and was rudely rebuffed by President Biden himself. Leaning into the podium with an air of arrogance that can only come with knowing that the corporate media machine is behind you 100 percent, KJP said, "That was, as I said, a cheap fake. It was definitely a cheap fake. It was! This was widely fact-checked, including by conservative media, including what happened, what occurred…. If you run that tape a little bit longer, you would see what is happening, what the president was actually doing, and it was a cheap fake!"

In other words, don't believe your lying eyes. Just believe what the White House tells you, and don't ask questions.

---

4   Tom Elliot, "Ladies and gentlemen, let's revisit this supercut from 12 days ago" X, June 28, 2024, https://x.com/mazemoore/status/180655678097917 5820?s=46&t=a5viIaTsjjnrqpqncjQvCg (accessed September 8, 2024).

5   Linskey and Hughes, "Behind Closed Doors, Biden Shows Signs of Slipping."

When CNN and other networks aired selectively edited footage of President Trump speaking about "a bloodbath" for the auto industry, making it seem like he was calling for *literal* murder, I didn't hear the term used once. The Biden White House only began using it—and the Mockingbird Media only began repeating it—because they knew that even accurate, unedited footage of Joe Biden would be enough to sow doubts about Biden's candidacy and lead straight to the reelection of President Trump.

Much like "misinformation," which the Biden administration attempted unsuccessfully to do away with early in their time in office, the term "cheap fake" simply translates to "true information Democrats don't want you to see." It means videos of Biden falling down, bumping into people, and struggling to find his way off stages. It means footage that should have appeared every night on the major news networks—whose job, we often forget, is to keep the American people informed about what is really going on with their government—if the corporate press weren't so hellbent on hiding it.

It wasn't until debate night, when the corporate press got caught, that things began to come crumbling down. The next morning, Joe Scarborough sat at his desk, nearly weeping, and admitted that Biden hadn't looked great. The same was true, as we've seen, of the Biden loyalists over at MSNBC. It was a sight that the United States hadn't seen since the night of the 2016 election, with every liberal cable news host in the country practically weeping on live television.

I, on the other hand, was glad that the truth had finally been revealed.

A little after 10:30 p.m., I hit the airwaves and delivered the debate wrap-up segment of my dreams. Everything my colleagues and I had been reporting for years had been revealed to the American people to be true, and not a "right-wing conspiracy," as the corporate media had been claiming all along.

All of these Biden-supporting networks, the media monsters who have shamelessly shielded this man from years of accountability, were forced to admit publicly what their anchors had been whispering to one another in private for years.

Biden is toast.

As former Trump advisor Stephen Miller said in the aftermath of the debate, "The biggest hoax in history has been exposed. Anybody who's anybody in the Democratic Party participated in, knew of, and covered up Biden's cognitive dysfunction while allowing secret unnamed staffers to run the country." That, of course, included the legacy media.

For a moment, it seemed that there might be a moment of reckoning for these networks. Perhaps now, they could begin reporting the truth rather than trying to do the impossible job of making Joe Biden look good all the time.

But that moment didn't last long.

The very next day, Joe Biden traveled to Philadelphia and sat for an interview with WURD Radio. Just hours later, it was revealed that Andrea Lawful-Sanders, the journalist who interviewed Biden, accepted pre-approved questions from the White House, then asked the questions as if she'd come up with them herself. This breach of journalistic ethics was too much even for the far-left editors at WURD Radio, who "parted ways" with Lawful-Sanders almost immediately. As Seb Gorka put it on *Newsline*, "this black woman is now out of a job, all thanks to Joe Biden!"

At least the folks at WURD had the guts to admit what they did.

ABC's George Stephanopoulos, on the other hand, still pretended to be objective as he guided Joe Biden through a softball interview after the debate, coddling him and jumping in whenever the president trailed off. It was only in private, on the streets of New York City, that Stephanopoulos admitted he didn't think Biden "could serve another four years," a comment that reportedly made an executive at ABC News "furious."[6] Just hours after the video hit the internet, Stephanopoulos had to express regret for accidentally telling the truth—which, apparently, is forbidden if you work for ABC News.

Imagine that. A man who became famous by destroying the reputations of victims of sexual assault to get Bill Clinton elected governor of Arkansas in the early '90s isn't exactly "objective" when it comes to helping Democrats. But he wasn't the only one. The newsroom of the *New York Times*, despite the calls coming from the paper's editorial board for Biden to drop out, began publishing cover stories again just a few days after the debate. One headline read, "For Joe Biden, What Seems Like Age Might Instead Be Style." The reporter A.O. Scott wrote that Biden's cognitive decline might simply be a "late style," similar to that of writers and musicians who, "at the end of their careers, enter a new and distinctive phase of creativity."

Are you kidding me? Oh yeah, naming dead leaders while our adversaries are watching. What a *vibe*. Sorry, Mr. Scott. This isn't *hot boy summer* at the old folks' home! This is not a look that flatters anyone. Let alone the leader of the free world.

The *coup de grace*, of course, came during a White House press briefing with Karine Jean-Pierre that June. After lying to the press about whether President Biden had seen a neurologist at the White House—a statement she'd walk back later in the day—the press secretary engaged in a perfectly normal, nothing-to-see-here shouting match with reporters. Then she took questions from friendly outlets, one of which—and I am not

---

6   Ivana Saric, "Stephanopoulos apologizes after saying Biden can't serve another term," Axios, July 10, 2024, https://www.axios.com/2024/07/10/george-stephanopoulos-biden-tmz-apology (accessed September 18, 2024).

making this up—was *this*, from a real, definitely-not-planted journalist in the back of the room:

"Do you have any concerns right now that this is the bleeding edge of a Russia effort to interfere in the election? Have you seen any evidence that the Russians have tried to seize on the debate performance to repeat some of the president's most embarrassing moments?"

"That's a very good question," said Karine Jean-Pierre.

These people never learn.

After years of pushing the debunked Russia hoax after Hillary Clinton lost in 2016, the media *really* seemed poised to try the same thing again. Even after they tried to convince us that the Hunter Biden laptop story—which was completely accurate, as anyone who's read Miranda Devine's *Laptop from Hell* knows—was "Russian disinformation," they haven't given up on trying to push this wild fantasy on the American people. When in doubt, I guess these old media institutions just start grasping around for what they know.

And what they know is *Russia, Russia, Russia.*

I guess we shouldn't have been surprised when, just a few days after that press conference, stories about how Hillary Clinton might do in a rematch against President Trump began popping up on cable news. The polling for Clinton, they said, looked good (which, of course, it also did in 2016, when she got the pantsuit beaten off of her on election night). The long-time Democrat strategist James Carville—the other half of the gruesome twosome that helped get Bill Clinton elected in the '90s—wrote an op-ed for the *New York Times* outlining his latest bright idea.

"Mark my words," he wrote. "Joe Biden is going to be out of the 2024 presidential race. Whether he is ready to admit it or not." To nominate a replacement, Carville suggested "four historic town halls" during the summer of 2024, moderated by "the two most obvious and qualified people in the world...

Barack Obama and Bill Clinton." Then Michelle Obama's name began re-appearing in news stories about potential replacements for Joe Biden.

For a second there, I had to wonder if I had tripped and fallen into a time machine that took me back to 2015, when the legacy press was telling us Donald Trump had less than a 1 percent chance of ever becoming president, and top aides to Hillary Clinton were buying houses in Washington, DC, because they were so sure they'd all be working in the White House come January 2017.

But no.

They were *really* going to try all this again.

The Russia hoax. The Obamas. The Clintons. Some last-minute October surprise that involved the intelligence community and bogus claims about President Trump. To some people, this would all seem like a rehash of the 2016 election. To me, it's just another go-around in a cycle that's been happening for almost forty years now. The legacy media attacks Republicans and covers for Democrats. When people point out that legacy media stories look an awful lot like the Democratic Party's talking points, the people in charge wave their hands and assure us there's nothing to see here.

But in recent years, the media's attacks on conservatives have crossed the line from merely crazy to unhinged and dangerous. During President Trump's time in office, many members of the legacy media began describing themselves as "The Resistance," a name typically associated with countries whose governments are under foreign occupation. These same people accused the president of being a dictator, a Russian asset, and a threat to democracy. They spoke as if they were begging someone to pick up a weapon and "resist" President Trump in person.

Like frogs in boiling water, most Americans probably didn't notice as the temperature of this rhetoric increased.

They got used to hearing ridiculous, overblown statements from the Democrats and their allies in the mainstream media. By the time Joe Biden said it was time to "put Donald Trump in the bullseye," the American public had become so desensitized that almost no one pointed it out.

Until it was too late.

You might wonder how we got to a place where one presidential candidate could say something like that about another one—especially without one of the country's legacy media networks saying a word about it.

It's a story nearly three decades in the making.

And I've had a front-row seat for all of it.

~

She's running.

I don't remember the first person who told me. But I remember being shocked. Hillary Clinton, former first lady of the United States, was going to run for an open Senate seat in New York, where she had been living for about four seconds at the time.

It was 1999, and I'd been in Albany for about two years, working my way up the ladder at WTEN, the local ABC station. In that time, I'd covered hundreds of press conferences, court cases, and crimes. I'd sharpened my skills, gathering the facts and reporting them, crafting stories that gave voters the information they needed to make decisions at the voting booth.

Now, I was going to report on a story that already had major national implications. Unlike her opponent, Hillary Clinton hadn't spent much time in the state of New York. To address the concerns of voters, her campaign organized a "listening tour" around the state, during which Hillary was supposed to hear the concerns of voters and make the case for her candidacy. As a relatively young reporter, I attended a few of these sessions. And what I saw taught me a great deal about the relationship between establishment Democrats and the legacy media. Which, for all intents and purposes, are really the same thing.

The Clinton campaign only allowed friendly reporters access to the candidate. Anyone who appeared to be objective was given the cold shoulder. Including me. So, with the support of the corporate press, Hillary Clinton won New York in a coronation that wouldn't be matched until Kamala Harris became the presidential nominee so many years later. She began her post-FLOTUS chapter and headed straight for the top of the Democrat Party's ticket.

I wasn't surprised. During my early years in journalism, I had been inspired by the tireless work of the few intrepid reporters who'd been willing to report accurately on the Clintons. As one woman after another came forward to say that Bill Clinton had sexually assaulted them, the legacy press pushed back hard. But a few journalists were willing to go against the mainstream narrative and investigate. The results soon made headlines all over the country. While in office, President Clinton had engaged in a sexual relationship with Monica Lewinsky, a White House intern.

In response, President Clinton's aides in the White House—including George Stephanopoulos, who'd later go on to pretend to be an objective journalist—got to work attacking these women savagely for coming forward. They'd made up outright lies and refused to comment on the four ongoing investigations. In the midst of that scandal, Hillary Clinton had gone on television and blamed the whole thing on a "vast right-wing conspiracy" against her husband. (Conveniently for them, the phrase "Believe All Women" hadn't been invented yet.)

Looking at that interview today, you can see the seeds of everything that would follow. The only difference was that back in the 1990s, the legacy media still had a few journalists willing to report the truth, even when the truth was bad for Democrats. Over the next few years, as Hillary Clinton ascended to the top ranks of the Democratic Party, that began to change. Maybe the media got the message during the administration of Barack Obama, who cracked down on press freedom in ways that even Richard Nixon wouldn't have dreamed up. During his eight years in office, according to James Risen of the *New York Times*, Barack Obama "spied on reporters by monitoring their phone records, labeled one journalist an unindicted co-conspirator in a criminal case for simply doing reporting, and issued subpoenas to other reporters to try to force them to reveal their sources and testify in criminal cases."[7]

One of these journalists was my colleague James Rosen who was indicted by the Obama administration because he reported on information leaked to him by the State Department. For years, journalists have relied on inside sources to report stories about the government and hold power to account. It was how the Pentagon Papers were released to the American public, telling the real story about the war in Vietnam. But when journalists do it to the wrong presidents—especially Obama—they end up labeled enemies of the state.

Speaking in 2017, when the media was in full freakout mode over Donald Trump's supposed war on the press, Rosen wrote for Fox News that the Obama administration had: "Literally, in writing declared me an enemy of the state by designating me as a criminal co-conspirator in an alleged

---

7   James Risen, "If Donald Trump Targets Journalists, Thank Obama," *The New York Times*," December 30, 2016, https://www.nytimes.com/2016/12/30/opinion/sunday/if-donald-trump-targets-journalists-thank-obama.html (accessed September 8, 2024).

violation of the Espionage Act. That was done in a secret FBI search warrant application submitted to and accepted and approved by a federal judge. Attorney General [Eric] Holder later acknowledged that he personally signed off on that document and he later identified it as the greatest regret of his tenure. Nothing that we've seen so far from the Trump administration, at least yet, rises to that level of seriousness or nature in terms of any kind of attack or assault on the press."

So: One side calls the media names; the other tries to put journalists in prison.

Guess which side the media believes is a unique threat to press freedom?

This quiet war on the press had real consequences. Journalists became afraid to cross the giant Democrat machine for fear that they'd have their careers destroyed. Not that many of them wanted to do it anyway. By the time Barack Obama got into the White House—with Hillary Clinton as his secretary of state and Joe Biden as his vice president—the journalism profession had entered a period of steep decline. Revenues were down. The ideological shift that had begun in the late '90s was complete. According to a survey conducted in 2013, more than 95 percent of journalists working in major newsrooms were registered Democrats. Despite claims of "objectivity," these reporters were willing to believe anything that mainstream Democrats like Barack Obama and Hillary Clinton told them.

It's not surprising that when Hillary Clinton claimed that Trump voters in the middle of the country were nothing more than "racists, sexists, and xenophobes" who constituted a "basket of deplorables," the media didn't call her out for using such dehumanizing rhetoric. In fact, they helped her double down. *The Atlantic* published a piece that said every person voting for Donald Trump was inherently racist and sexist. For NBC News, a writer named Stephen Nuño-Pérez wrote a piece titled "Hillary is Wrong. 100 Percent of Trump Voters are Deplorable."[8] This blatant hatred for half the country would have been unthinkable in the 1990s, when major news organizations at least pretended to be objective.

But things had changed. As younger, more sensitive reporters began filling the lower ranks at our legacy media institutions, things got woke very fast. Suddenly, kids who'd been educated in critical race theory and Marxism at our nation's universities were calling the shots. Producers and editors found themselves dealing with a new generation of reporters who believed that journalists should act more like left-wing political activists than objective purveyors of the truth. So, when the Clinton campaign came to them with a crazy conspiracy theory about Donald Trump, they were happy to pick it up and run with it, no questions asked.

Looking back, we can see exactly what happened. Early in her campaign for president, Hillary Clinton got word that her past ties to Russia might be a problem with voters. According to a recent report by Jeff Gerth in the *Columbia Journalism Review*, the campaign was extremely worried about several Clinton-Russia links unearthed by a collaboration between the conservative author Peter Schweizer and the *New York Times*, "including a lucrative speech in Moscow by Bill Clinton, Russia-related donations to the Clinton family foundation, and Russia-friendly initiatives by the Obama administration while Hillary was secretary of state.... An internal Clinton campaign poll, shared within the campaign the day of Trump's announcement [for president], showed that the Russia entanglements exposed in the book and the *Times* were

---

8   Stephen Nuño-Pérez, "Opinion: Hillary is Wrong. 100 Percent of Trump Voters are Deplorable," NBC News, September 10, 2016, https://www.nbcnews.com/news/latino/opinion-hillary-wrong-100-percent-trump-voters-are-deplorable-n646156 (accessed September 18, 2024).

the most worrisome 'Clinton negative message,' according to campaign records."[9]

So, Hillary Clinton fell back on the advice of the radical writer Saul Alinsky, whose work on political organizing was extremely influential on the left-wing mobs that overran college campuses and public events in the 1960s. As a senior at Wellesley College, Clinton had written a ninety-two-page thesis on the man's work, which included a small book titled *Rules for Radicals*. One of those rules, familiar to left-wing dissidents everywhere, is: "Accuse your opponent of what you are doing, to create confusion and to inculcate voters against evidence of your own guilt."

By the time President Trump won the White House in late 2016, the Russia-collusion hoax had been picked up by every major media institution in the country. And the results were stunning. The theory had become so mainstream, in fact, that on January 6, 2017 (a date we don't hear about nearly as often as we should), eleven Democrat lawmakers publicly refused to certify the results of the election. Speaking from the floor of Congress, Representative Jim McGovern of Massachusetts said, "The electors were not lawfully certified, especially given the confirmed and illegal activities engaged by the government of Russia." Representative Maxine Waters of California tried the same thing. But they were both forced to stand down when they couldn't get any support from senators for their ridiculous Russia-collusion objections.

And it was all a lie, as anyone with a functioning brain could tell. But that didn't stop the media from pushing a narrative on the American people that the new president had been installed by Vladimir Putin, making him the most serious

---

9   Jeff Gerth, "The press versus the president, part one," *Columbia Journalism Review*, January 30, 2023, https://www.cjr.org/special_report/trumped-up-press-versus-president-part-1.php (accessed September 8, 2024).

threat to democracy in the history of the country. During the four years President Trump was in office, the media saw themselves not as objective purveyors of the truth, but as a movement dedicated to stopping the president's agenda at all costs.

In addition, the stories that were published about Trump voters made Hillary Clinton's "basket of deplorables" comment seem kind by comparison. Viewing footage of people lining up outside a Trump rally, the political consultant Rick Wilson laughed with CNN's Anderson Cooper about how poor and presumably stupid those people were. When Special Counsel John Durham released his report detailing all the shadowy tricks that the FBI and other intelligence agencies had played to get Donald Trump—and there were *many*—the corporate press attempted to brush it all under the rug.

But before that happened, the legacy media gave themselves tons of prizes for their coverage of the Russia hoax. From 2017 to 2019, most of the Pulitzer Prizes—which are given out by the journalism school at Columbia University, mostly to people who've attended the school or taught there—went to reporters covering some aspect of the Trump-Russia collusion story. To this day, those prizes hang on the walls at our nation's legacy media institutions—although, given President Trump's recently announced lawsuit against the Pulitzer Prize Board, they might not be hanging there much longer.

Rather than admitting that they had engaged in the biggest case of journalistic malpractice in American history, however, most organizations doubled down. They attempted to brush the Russia story under the rug, searching for the next thing that would get President Trump out of office. During the COVID-19 pandemic, the media worked overtime against the president. When he suggested, correctly, that the virus might have leaked from a lab in Wuhan, China, they called him a racist. When he shut down travel from China, they called him a racist.

Nothing, it seemed, could get in the way of the legacy media's narrative. In their eyes, President Trump was a white supremacist who had, despite mounting evidence to the contrary, been installed by Russian intelligence services so that he could usher the United States into an era of racism and fascism. Any positive stories about President Trump were buried. In October 2020, when the legacy media got word about a laptop belonging to Hunter Biden that contained salacious material about a leading presidential candidate, they pretended it didn't exist. And when the *New York Post*, one of the few credible newspapers left in the country, *did* report on the laptop's contents, the censorship team at Twitter locked the newspaper out of its account, banning anyone who shared the story, even in private messages. When President Trump attempted to bring up the laptop in a presidential debate, host Chris Wallace shut him down, probably altering the outcome of the election. And Chris Wallace felt so confident about this because fifty-one members of the United States intelligence community—none of whom have been disciplined or had their credentials revoked—said the laptop had "all the earmarks of Russian disinformation."

While this was happening, many Americans wondered how censorship had become so common. One answer is that large, for-profit companies had "colluded" (to use one of the Left's favorite words) to tamp down speech that might help Donald Trump regain the White House. In 2018, a private company called NewsGuard appeared, promising to root out "fake news" and rate journalistic organizations according to their credibility. The problem, of course, was that the people affiliated with this company—twenty of whom had donated to Democrat candidates in the past—had their own whacky ideas about what "fake news" was.

During the pandemic, the organization awarded low credibility scores to media outlets that took seriously the proposition that the virus might have come from a lab. Apparently, that was a "fake news conspiracy theory." These days, when even the Biden administration has been forced to admit that the virus probably *did* leak from a Chinese lab, those credibility scores haven't been restored. NewsGuard is waging an all-out economic war on conservative outlets, ruthlessly targeting them under the guise of combating the latest "conspiracy theory"—which, let's be real, often just means "a truth you're not allowed to say yet." This isn't a coincidence; it's a calculated assault, bolstered by funding from none other than the Biden administration's State Department and other government agencies. With the Democrats pulling the strings, NewsGuard is using its influence to silence voices that dare to challenge their narrative, crippling conservative media with financial strangulation. This is not just censorship; it's a coordinated effort to crush dissent and monopolize the flow of information, ensuring that only the Left's version of "truth" sees the light of day.

In February 2024, I had Congressman Jim Banks on *Newsline*, just after he had sent a letter to the CEOs of top advertising agencies warning them about NewsGuard. After thanking me for having him on the show, he said, "NewsGuard, as we already know, is a left-wing think tank and we know that they censor conservative outlets like your own.... NewsGuard actually says that the *China Daily*, a newspaper owned by the Chinese Communist Party, is more reputable than Newsmax. So that's how terrible an organization NewsGuard is." He also noted that the American Federation of Teachers Unions signed an agreement in 2022 that allowed it to use media monitors in schools. Congressman Banks said, "ATF has decided that NewsGuard, whose leadership falsely dismissed the Hunter Biden laptop story as 'Russian disinformation,' deserves to be empowered to tell children what is and isn't 'misinformation.'"

Fortunately, there are a few other people willing to fight against such blatant censorship. During an interview on *Newsline* in January 2024, Jimmy Patronis, the chief financial officer of Florida, said, "The state of Florida spends a lot of money advertising. We have made it loud and clear through my agency bill that we are not going to allow any taxpayer dollars to go to any news service that subscribes to NewsGuard. We're not going to allow this restrictive movement that is putting the conservative opinion out of the public light."

Over the past few years, the legacy media has had many chances to do a full accounting of what has gone wrong. They could have done what the *New York Times* did after its botched reporting on weapons of mass destruction in Iraq, firing the reporter responsible and combing through every line of the bad stories. But they have refused to do it repeatedly, choosing instead to double down on their worst lies, hoping that giant censorship firms like NewsGuard will help them paper over their worst mistakes.

Their mission was to help Joe Biden and hurt Donald Trump. And the worse things got for Joe Biden—the more he stumbled, stared off into space, and failed to help average Americans out of the many problems they were facing—the more left-wing journalists had to bend their code of ethics to make him look good.

And as the summer of 2024 wore on, it became clear just how far those ethical rules could bend before they finally snapped.

❧

In American journalism, there are a few hard and fast rules. For instance, you can't pay sources for information (no matter what the guy who took over the *Washington Post* for a few days tells you). You can't pull a Claudine Gay and lift lines directly from other stories without attribution.

Most important, you can *never* accept pre-written questions from a person you're interviewing, no matter how much you might like them personally.

That is what PR firms do. It's not what journalists do.

But in 2024, when the world is apparently "on the verge of slipping into a fascist dictatorship" (according to MSNBC), the rules for our liberal media are a little different. On July 11, for instance, during Joe Biden's attempted post-debate cleanup tour, it was revealed that "in appearance after appearance [over the past two years], the president has been served up nearly identical questions, prescreened or suggested ahead of time by campaign staff members. And in nearly every case, the questions set the president up to deliver on-message talking points, without notable flubs."[10] These questions, which were asked by supposedly independent radio and television hosts all over the country, included, "What are your accomplishments?" and "What is at stake for Black Americans in this upcoming election?"[11]

Around the same time, a radio station in Milwaukee admitted that it had honored a request by the Biden administration to cut out two gaffes from a recent interview with the president before airing it. The station apologized and said it would make the full interview—including the gaffes it had cut—available online.

Which were, according to the *Milwaukee Journal Sentinel*:

1. At time of 5:20, the removal of "...and in addition to that, I have more blacks in my administration than

---

10   Ken Bensinger, "Biden Campaign Has Long Fed Softball Questions to Friendly Interviewers," *The New York Times*, July 11, 2024, https://www.nytimes.com/2024/07/11/us/politics/biden-campaign-media-2024.html?smid=nytcore-ios-share&referringSource=articleShare&sgrp=c-cb (accessed September 8, 2024).

11   Ibid.

any other president, all other presidents combined, and in major positions, cabinet positions."

2. At time 14:15, in reference to Donald Trump's call for the death penalty for the Central Park Five, the removal of "I don't know if they even call for their hanging or not, but he—but they said [...] convicted of murder."[12]

These aren't the kinds of things you remove from an interview because they're beside the point. In an interview with the president of the United States, *nothing* he says is beside the point. They're the kind of things you remove because you're worried they're going to make your guy look crazy and addled.

Now, I hate to always play the "what if this were President Trump" game, because doing that can drive you crazy. But seriously! What if that *had* been President Trump? If *he* had spoken that way during an interview with the legacy media, those quotes would have been in the headline. The *Washington Post* would have added two more "lies" to its bogus running tally of all the untruths President Trump supposedly told while in office. MSNBC's Rachel Maddow would have done a full hour on the president's use of the word "murder," telling her viewers that it proved President Trump had secretly been the Zodiac Killer all along.

Bear in mind that these radio stations didn't come clean about what they'd done because of a guilty conscience or out of some sense of civic duty. They did it because they got caught. And if they *hadn't* gotten caught—if Joe Biden hadn't proven himself to be a mumbling mess in front of fifty million

---

12 Jessie Opoien and Molly Beck, "Milwaukee radio station says it agreed to edit interview with Joe Biden," *Milwaukee Journal Sentinel*, July 11, 2024, https:// www.jsonline.com/story/news/politics/elections/2024/07/11/milwaukee-radio-station-says-it-agreed-to-edit-interview-with-biden/74369012007/ (accessed September 8, 2024).

Americans during the debate on June 27—the world might never have found out just how deeply rotted our legacy media institutions have become. Concerns about Joe Biden's age might have remained "right-wing conspiracy theories" forever. White House aides would have been able to keep up Operation "Bubble Wrap" (the name that they *actually* used for the practice of keeping Biden out of the spotlight) until election night.

But they got caught, and our legacy media was exposed for what it was. Again, this could have prompted some reflection, especially among the pundits who had assured us that this Biden was "the best Biden ever." But it didn't. These anchors continued attacking President Trump and defending their old, decrepit candidate. In mid-July, after facing scathing criticism from readers for calling on Joe Biden to drop out of the race, the *New York Times* editorial board published a bleak, apocalyptic editorial titled "HE IS UNFIT." And they weren't talking about Biden. The cover image showed President Trump against a black background, warning readers about all the ways he might violate the United States Constitution if he won a second term. Similar rhetoric could be heard on all liberal media networks, which simply could not face the fact that they had been exposed.

It's no wonder that President Trump, speaking to Jeff Gerth of the *Columbia Journalism Review* in 2021, said, "I realized early on I had two jobs. The first was to run the country, and the second was survival. I had to survive: the stories were unbelievably fake."

Back then, the word "survive" might have seemed metaphorical. Few people would have believed that the fake news actually wanted President Trump dead. But to those of us who'd been paying attention, his use of the word seemed downright chilling. Even after President Trump was out of office, the media continued its assault on the man and his legacy. They cheered on several baseless prosecutions of him by the Biden administration, failing to apply any real scrutiny to the facts surrounding the cases. They wrote stories about President Trump that compared him to dictators, warning the American public that if he ever returned to power, democracy would end. The man, they assured us, was dangerous.

In October 2023, an opinion writer for the *New York Times* wrote an article titled "Donald Trump is going to get someone killed," predicting that soon, an insane Republican who'd been "radicalized" by President Trump's tough rhetoric would pick up a gun and kill someone. During the summer of 2024, *The New Republic* published a full issue with President Trump's face superimposed onto an old campaign poster of Adolf Hitler, tiny moustache and all. The message was clear. In the eyes of our legacy media, Donald Trump was as bad as Hitler. Something needed to be done about him.

It was only a matter of time before someone took this ridiculous rhetoric seriously. This was always going to end with what the legacy media might call a "violent, but mostly peaceful assassination attempt."

Which, on July 13, 2024, is exactly what happened.

FIGHT, FIGHT, FIGHT!

I t was a sunny summer day in July, and the crowd at the rally was electric. President Trump, dressed in a suit and his signature red MAGA hat, was just beginning to lay into the finer points of his plan for a second term.

"If you want to really see something that's sad," he said, turning to a chart that showed the sky-high illegal immigration rates under Joe Biden, "take a look at what happened—"

Shots rang out. Screams erupted from the crowd. President Trump raised a hand to his right ear and scanned his surroundings, as if searching for someone to attack. He hit the deck. Men and women in black suits piled on top of him, forming a human shield. In a matter of seconds, the shooter—who'd set up on the roof of a nearby building—was dead. President Trump fought his way back to his feet and told his Secret Service detail to wait while he put his shoes back on. The right side of his face was stained with blood.

A would-be assassin's bullet had pierced his right ear.

At this point, most men—certainly most presidents— would have allowed themselves to be carried off by the Secret Service and stuffed into a car. But President Trump, as we all know, is different. Rather than remaining on the ground and hiding behind the armed men tasked with saving his life, the once and future president of the United States raised his fist in defiance, pumping it toward the crowd and yelling "FIGHT,

FIGHT, FIGHT!" Chants of "USA! USA!" erupted even as rallygoers scrambled to file out of the event space, which had just become the scene of the first attempted presidential assassination since President Ronald Reagan was shot outside the Washington Hilton in 1981. As he was taken offstage by his protective detail, President Trump raised his fist again. An image of the pose taken by Doug Mills, a *New York Times* photographer, soon made its way around the world.

History had been made.

The initial response from the media was, of course, to downplay what had happened. A CNN headline read, "Secret Service rushes Trump offstage after he falls at rally." Another in the *Washington Post* read, "Trump escorted away after loud noises at Pa. rally." A document that circulated around social media in the wake of the attack contained guidance from a news director cautioning anchors to "be mindful of body language when presenting the story. No need for 'serious' face or adding comments and adjectives for color. No need to say 'scary moments today at a Trump rally....' Just get to the story."

But the images captured that evening told the story in a way no reporter ever could. One showed President Trump on the ground, hands clasped, almost as if in prayer. Another showed him seconds later, back on his feet and ready to go again. In the days to come, the world learned what most of us had known for years: that this man is truly unstoppable. Nothing, not even a bullet, was going to get between him and the presidency.

The profile of the shooter was predictable, if slightly strange. A disaffected loner looking to get famous, who was somehow able to climb onto the roof within shooting distance of the former president of the United States despite the protection of the supposed best security force in the world.

It was only a matter of time. For years, Joe Biden and the Democrats had been attacking President Trump with extreme, outlandish rhetoric. And they pretended *he* was the one using the heated language. Consider what happened when President Trump said that a second Biden administration would usher in a "bloodbath" for the auto industry. Within minutes, every corporate media outlet in the country had run with the quote, purposely omitting any mention of the auto industry to make it seem like President Trump had been threatening literal murder. Rather than write a story about how the Biden administration's electric vehicle mandates were going to destroy the American auto industry—which was what President Trump had meant—they ran stories attempting to convince us that he wanted to be a dictator. They told us that his election would mean the end of democracy as we know it. They said elections would end, and that President Trump would be a dictator. A writer for the *Washington Post* wrote a long essay comparing Donald Trump to Julius Caesar, stating that it was time to "stop pretending" about the threat the former president posed. Hardly a day went by without someone on the Left comparing President Trump to Hitler on television.

In the aftermath of the attempted assassination, Joe Biden spoke about the need to stop using such heated rhetoric and come together as a country.

Please.

Just weeks earlier, while recovering from his disastrous debate performance, Joe Biden suggested it was time to put President Trump "in the bullseye." A few months earlier, Democrats in Congress had attempted to revoke President Trump's Secret Service protection.[1] Hours after the shooting, a source told *The Federalist* that Trump's campaign had made repeated requests to the Biden administration to increase the

---

1   H.R. 8081, DISGRACED Former Protectees Act, 118th Cong. https://www.congress.gov/bill/118th-congress/house-bill/8081/text?s=1&r=3 (accessed September 8, 2024).

number of Secret Service agents on President Trump's detail. But they were "rebuffed time and again by Biden's DHS."[2] Alejandro Mayorkas flatly denied this fact several times on television. Of course, it would later prove to be true.

The moment of reckoning came when Kimberly Cheatle, the Secret Service director, testified before Congress about the failures of her agency. Just days earlier, Senator Marsha Blackburn came on *Newsline* and spoke to me about the momentous event. Speaking not long after she'd been in the room, Senator Blackburn said, "They identified a suspicious person an hour before Donald Trump was shot. [At] 5:51 [p.m.] they knew he was a potential threat. [At] 5:53 [p.m.] the sharpshooters are alerted, but yet at 6 [p.m.], Secret Service cleared Donald Trump to go on that stage. Now, the Trump campaign needs answers, the Trump family and the American people want answers. And, as you have seen today, Kimberly Cheatle is not willing to provide those answers. When she's not willing to give answers, I think that what we have to do is look at this and say, What is she hiding and why is she not more forthcoming? There should have been an advanced planning document. There should have been an operational document. We should be able to know who was participating in what capacity. She doesn't even know the answer to how many agents were actually on the ground."

Shortly after her testimony, the Secret Service director resigned. In August 2024, bodycam footage revealed the extent of the serious failure of the Secret Service. In the video, one local officer can be heard shouting, "I told them they need to post guys over there," referring to the spot on the roof where the shooter was able to mount his rifle and shoot President

---

2   Sean Davis, "BREAKING: A source familiar with Trump's security detail…," X, July 13, 2024, https://x.com/seanmdav/status/1812278386514870623 (accessed September 8, 2024).

Trump. "I told them on Tuesday. I talked to the Secret Service guys, they were like, 'Yeah, no problem, we're going to post guys over here.'"

By the time this book is released, I'm sure we'll know even more about the Secret Service's actions on that day. And I'm sure Democrats will do everything in their power to *keep* us from finding out about it.

I'm not surprised. For years now, the Biden-Harris White House has been attempting to make President Trump go away. First, they did it by banning him from social media. When that didn't work, they attempted to put him in prison. When even *that* didn't work, they filled the public square with dangerous, toxic rhetoric about how he was a unique threat to democracy that needed to be stopped by any means necessary. And of course, the legacy media parroted their talking points. And they knew their voters would listen. According to a recent study conducted by a political scientist at the University of Chicago, researchers found that 10 percent of people surveyed "said that the 'use of force is justified to prevent Donald Trump from becoming president.' A third of those who gave that answer also said they owned a gun."

Like I said: It was only a matter of time.

And the Democrats knew it.

For years now, the radical Left has been losing.

And they haven't exactly been taking it well.

When President Trump nominated a mild-mannered federal judge named Brett Kavanaugh to replace Justice Anthony Kennedy on the Supreme Court, mobs of left-wing activists lost their minds. Within days, they had concocted a fanciful narrative painting Justice Kavanaugh as a gang rapist, using a confused woman named Christine Blasey-Ford as a weapon to score points against Republicans. The woman's story didn't make any sense, and the details she gave were scattered at best. But that didn't stop Democrats from questioning Judge Kavanaugh for hours, telling lurid tales of disgusting high school antics that weren't even close to true. The spectacle, watched by millions of people around the country over three days, was unlike anything we had ever witnessed.

In the end, Justice Kavanaugh was confirmed. He took his seat on the Supreme Court. But the damage to his reputation had been done. Just days after he took the stand to defend himself, speaking through tears, Matt Damon mocked him on *Saturday Night Live*. The studio audience roared with laughter during the routine, which involved ridiculous fake crying and sniffling. In the months that followed, several legacy media publications relaxed their fact-checking standards to publish *more* unfounded allegations about Brett Kavanaugh. Hawaii Senator Mazie Hirono, who'd piled on during the worst of the Kavanaugh hearings, delighted as she told reporters that Justice Kavanaugh would always "have an asterisk next to his name."

In the eyes of these Democrat lawmakers—as well as the millions of far-left radicals in newsrooms around the country who pushed these baseless allegations to get clicks—what they were doing was justified. If Brett Kavanaugh got on the Supreme Court, he might rule in a way they didn't like. He would, as one columnist for the *Washington Post* put it, "usher in an era of instability and fascism on the Supreme Court." During this time, it was common for images from the dystopian sci-fi series *The Handmaid's Tale* to appear on Twitter, grimly predicting the future we could all expect under a conservative Supreme Court. Women would become property. Evil white men would enslave everyone.

Again, it was only a matter of time before some insane left-wing activist took matters into his (or her, or their, or zim/zer) own hands.

Which is exactly what happened on June 8, 2022, when a young man from California traveled to the home of Brett Kavanaugh armed with a "'black tactical chest rig and a tactical knife,' a pistol with two magazines and ammunition, pepper spray, zip ties, a hammer, a screwdriver, a nail punch, a crowbar, a pistol light, and duct tape." As this man stepped out of a taxi in front of Justice Kavanaugh's house, he happened to spot two federal marshals in a car. He walked the other direction down the street and called his sister, who suggested he call 911. A few hours later, he was arrested.

There had been a bill on the House floor to provide extra security to justices. But Nancy Pelosi allowed it to languish. As Senator Mike Braun told me on my show, "House Speaker Nancy Pelosi is doing what she normally does by keeping a bill to protect the Supreme Court justices waiting," even after this alarming incident. Braun emphasized the urgency of protecting justices in their own homes, especially considering that Pelosi had previously downplayed the threat by saying, "nobody is in danger over the weekend."

Now, if those two federal marshals had been parked a block away rather than right in front of the house (or if they had failed to guard the house altogether, like the Secret Service agents in charge of protecting President Trump in Butler, Pennsylvania), the night might have ended differently. The next day's *New York Times* might have featured Justice Kavanaugh's obituary on the front page rather than the four-sentence blurb about the assassination attempt that it ended up printing (on page A20, by the way). The country might have had its reckoning with the heated rhetoric of the radical Left much earlier— maybe early enough to save President Trump from being shot at during the summer of 2024.

But probably not. If the reaction to the attempted assassination of Brett Kavanaugh tells us anything, it's that the media will never care about political violence if that violence cannot be used to further a left-wing agenda. I can only imagine the headlines we would have seen the next day if it had been Sonya Sotomayor, or Ruth Bader Ginsberg, who'd been stalked by a would-be assassin. It would have been similar to the all-hands-on-deck outrage that we saw in the aftermath of January 6, when hundreds of peaceful protestors were rounded up and given extremely harsh (and unlawful) prison sentences with terrorism enhancements.

The same, no doubt, would have happened if it had been Joe Biden, not Donald Trump, who'd been shot in the ear on July 13. We would have known the shooter's motive immediately, and that motive—somehow—would have been white supremacy. President Trump would have been blamed for his heated rhetoric in a way that Democrats never are. And we'd have new laws tamping down on what we are allowed to say.

But it wasn't Joe Biden. It was Donald Trump, who took the bullet in stride and got back on his feet with his fist raised at the crowd. As such, the media will probably have forgotten the shooter's name by the time this book reaches your hands.

Quick.

Without looking it up, do you remember it?

I'm willing to bet you didn't. The same probably goes for the person who almost killed Brett Kavanaugh. Or the crazed Bernie Bro who loaded up his automatic weapon and opened fire on Republicans at the Congressional Baseball Game in 2017, almost killing Representative Steve Scalise. The names of these people don't often make headlines because they don't fit the legacy media's narrative about political violence in America—which, according to the talking heads at MSNBC and CNN, is that violence only ever occurs when white supremacists in MAGA hats do it. Whenever there's an altercation between a black man and police, the world stops, and the cable networks devote twenty-four/seven coverage to it. Opinion anchors use the story to prove that the United

States really is a systemically racist country in which things are worse than they've ever been.

When similar altercations happen that don't fit the narrative, no one hears about them. I'm sure, for instance, that most Americans don't know the name Tony Timpa. In Dallas, Texas, in November 2016, Timpa (who is white) was pulled over by police and thrown to the ground, where an officer held his knee on Timpa's neck for a full eight minutes. Timpa called out for his mother before he died. But the world didn't stop when it happened. There were no protests in the streets. In the eyes of the legacy media, Tony Timpa's death wasn't a big deal because it wasn't useful to them. It didn't reinforce the woke narrative that the United States is a systemically racist country full of MAGA-hatted white supremacists who roam the streets looking for minorities to oppress. As always, it's not just what the media cover; it's what they *don't* cover that really matters.

I'm sure almost no viewers of the legacy media will recall the name of the man who, in December 2021, got behind the wheel of a car in Waukesha, Wisconsin, and drove through a parade, killing six people and injuring dozens more. They won't know it because the man—whose name was Darrell Brooks, by the way—was not a white supremacist. And given that he was a black man who'd posted hateful things about white people on his Facebook page, they couldn't even pull their usual trick of calling him "white supremacist adjacent." So, they buried the story. Headlines on CNN told us that "a car" had plowed into all those people; an article on MSNBC said that "a white SUV" had killed six people.

The same is true of all the people who were arrested for killing and injuring police officers during all those "mostly peaceful" protests that occurred during the summer of 2020. It's true of the man (also non-white) who opened fire on a subway car in Brooklyn in April 2022. To this day, I'm sure people remember the names of the mass shooters who *did* fit the media's narrative. What they don't remember are the names of the supposedly loving, accepting people on the Left who turn to violence the second they don't get what they want.

Around the same time Brett Kavanaugh was almost assassinated, mobs of left-wing activists tore through the streets of our cities, throwing bricks through windows and spray-painting threats on buildings. One of these groups, which called itself Jane's Revenge (after the plaintiff of the original *Roe v. Wade* Supreme Court case) wrote variations of the message, "If abortions aren't safe, then neither are you" on buildings all over the country. In some cities, it was accompanied by anarchy signs and obscene drawings.

The message was clear. And it was the same message that the would-be assassin of Brett Kavanaugh wanted to send.

Do what we want, or else…

In today's America, these people feel comfortable making threats like this. They know that no matter what they do, the justice system—especially at the local level—will treat them with kid gloves. Unlike the grannies who showed up waving flags at the Capitol on January 6, 2021 (several of whom are now serving prison sentences), these left-wing terrorists will never get what they deserve. They certainly won't get it from the legacy media, who will bury any fact that doesn't align with the Democratic Party's talking points. But they also won't get it from our justice system—which, over the past few years, has been completely remade in the image of people who want to tear this country down from the inside out. Today, shoplifting has effectively become legal in our major cities as courts refuse to prosecute people for it; criminals are allowed out on bail after they've just committed serious crimes. People do not feel safe walking down the streets of the places where they've lived for years.

The rule of law no longer applies.

And it's not an accident.

In fact, this weakening of our justice system is all part of a plan. And today, as we head into the most consequential election season in the history of this country, that plan is beginning to come to fruition.

In the summer of 2016, while the world's pundits were focused on the upcoming presidential race (and Joe Biden, only about 136 years old at the time, was privately fuming that he hadn't yet been chosen to run for president), billionaire financier George Soros was writing checks. In the lead-up to that race, according to *Politico*, Soros had "channeled more than $3 million into seven local district-attorney campaigns in six states…a sum that [exceeded] all but a handful of rival super-donors."

For the most part, people don't think about their district attorneys. Until I became a news reporter in Albany covering the biggest players in New York politics, I didn't even give much thought to the power they held, but it is immense. When crimes are committed in their jurisdictions, they decide how to prosecute those crimes on behalf of the government. When it comes to *how* they prosecute crimes, as Thomas Hogan of *City Journal* has pointed out, "the U.S. Constitution and rules of criminal procedure establish a series of checks and balances that act to constrain the powers of the prosecutor (for example, indictment or preliminary-hearing requirements, the exclusionary rule for illegally obtained evidence, appeals, and so on." However, as George Soros and his goons overseas realized, prosecutors are "almost completely unconstrained in their ability to decide *not* to prosecute a defendant, regardless of the facts or the law."

In other words, district attorneys decide what cases will end up in court and which ones won't. They decide which defendants will be charged with crimes and which ones will walk free. And Soros—who seems to have something against law and order, as well as the United States of America in general—only wanted people who were going to let criminals walk free. In 2016, every candidate he backed had some very strange ideas about crime.

Specifically, that it was great, and people should be able to do it all the time without consequences.

In Philadelphia, Soros backed Larry Krasner, who believed that district attorneys should be concerned primarily with "social justice." That meant refusing to prosecute little things like, oh, I don't know, drug possession and shootings if the people who committed those crimes were non-white. As soon as Krasner took office, the rate at which gun crimes were dismissed in the city rose from 17 percent to 61 percent. The murder rate rose more than 200 percent. During Krasner's election night party in 2018, supporters chanted "F**k the FOP [the fraternal order of Police]" and "No good cops in a racist system."[3] As soon as Krasner took office, he fired thirty-one veteran prosecutors and issued a memo telling the assistant DAs in his office to "decline to charge four categories of crimes," to "charge lower gradations of crimes," and to "divert more cases, including drug distribution."

During his tenure, the city collapsed. The neighborhood of Kensington, where drug distribution and possession were effectively legal thanks to Krasner's policies, began to look like a scene out of *The Walking Dead*. Drug addicts stumbled

---

3   Charles "Cully" Stimson and Zack Smith, "Meet Larry Krasner, the Rogue Prosecutor Wreaking Havoc in Philadelphia," Heritage Foundation, October 29, 2020, https://www.heritage.org/crime-and-justice/commentary/meet-larry-krasner-the-rogue-prosecutor-wreaking-havoc-philadelphia (accessed September 8, 2024).

around with sores on their arms from shared needles, their teeth falling out of their mouths, and their bodies growing unbelievably thin from a lack of nutrition. Parents walked through the streets in search of kids who'd come to the neighborhood months earlier and disappeared into the underground network of tents and shelters. The scene became so bad that the government of Mexico (yes, *that* Mexico), a country that the US State Department warns its citizens about traveling to, used footage from Kensington in a television commercial warning its citizens about the dangers of drugs. The irony was stark: A nation that Americans are cautioned against visiting was now warning its own citizens about the dangers lurking on American streets.

During the summer of 2023, a reporter for Turning Point USA named Savanah Hernandez took to the streets of Kensington to film a person-on-the-street piece about a new needle exchange program that the city of Philadelphia was doing. Almost immediately, she was attacked by drug addicts on camera. Speaking on Newsmax shortly after the incident, she said, "This is happening on a public corner in the middle of America. This isn't a third world country. This is Philadelphia. Anyone can go and see this."

Luckily, Savanah Hernandez got out of the situation without any serious injuries, and she got some excellent footage along the way. Her work is a testament to what brave young journalists can do when they get out on the street and shine a light on what's really happening in our major cities. That's how I was raised in the business.

And lately, there's plenty to see. In almost every city that has been flooded with Soros money over the past decade, things have gotten downright apocalyptic. As soon as the first wave of Soros prosecutors took office, liberal cities experienced the largest single-year increase in homicides in American history. Not surprisingly, that increase occurred in 2020, when left-wing mobs were free to roam the streets destroying private property and police stations without fear that they'd ever be prosecuted for it. In fact, they were *encouraged* to do it by left-wing celebrities and activists, who set up charities to provide bail money for rioters. The next year, the murder rate ticked up even further. It happened in Chicago, where Kim Foxx became district attorney with the help of George Soros and began decriminalizing serious offenses. It happened in San Francisco, where Chesa Boudin, whose parents were *literally* left-wing terrorists in the '60s, took charge and instituted a pro-criminal agenda.

The damage is clear. All you have to do is walk around the streets of San Francisco, Chicago, or Baltimore (where Marilyn Mosby, another Soros prosecutor, made it legal to steal and sell drugs as much as you want), and you'll see that all this "social justice" stuff doesn't work. In fact, the communities hurt most by this kind of nonsense are usually the ones that are primarily inhabited by "people of color," the very citizens that Soros prosecutors claim they want to protect.

Recently, many of these prosecutors have been voted out of office. But the damage they've done still lingers. The next time you have to ring the bell at CVS to get a bottle of shampoo, you can thank the people who effectively made shoplifting legal. Every day, we see new videos of people leaving convenience stores with carts full of items, often walking right past security guards who know that arresting these criminals simply isn't worth it anymore. Within just a few days, they'll be back out on the streets. And if you dare to try and stop them and you happen to work for Lululemon, you'll be fired— something that actually happened to employees in Georgia.

Of course, not all the Soros prosecutors are gone. Alvin Bragg, for instance, who got just north of one million dollars from Soros during his campaign for district attorney of New York City in 2021, still has his job. And if you've taken a walk around Manhattan lately, you probably know how *that's* been going. Every day in that city, serious crimes occur with startling frequency. And the perpetrators, many of them migrants, aren't punished. According to the most recent statistics, instances of rape in New York City have risen 11 percent this year.[4] Carjackings are up 15 percent.[5]

It's the kind of thing that a district attorney might want to take a look at. But Alvin Bragg seems to believe that things like rape, robbery, and murder aren't worth his time. He seems more interested in becoming the first district attorney to successfully prosecute a former president, and it doesn't matter how many laws and norms he has to shatter to do it.

When Alvin Bragg first announced that he was about to indict President Trump in April 2023, my first reaction was, *Here we go. They are really going to do this!* In some sense, I had always known it could happen. But it was still shocking. I had been covering the legal system's war on Donald Trump for months, and I knew as well as anyone that the New York case was dead. It consisted of a few alleged campaign finance violations that the Federal Election Commission had already reviewed and declined to prosecute.

But Alvin Bragg, who up until that point had never met a criminal he wouldn't let off with a warning, performed legal gymnastics to create a case to go after President Trump. The indictment he ended up filing contained thirty-four separate

---

4   Tina Moore and Georgia Worrell, "Rape surges 11% in NYC—as bail reform, vulnerable migrants depleted NYPD create perfect crime storm," *New York Post,* July 20, 2024, https://nypost.com/2024/07/20/us-news/rape-surges-11-in-nyc/#:~:text=The%20Big%20Apple%20has%20seen,last%20year%2C%20NYPD%20stats%20reveal (accessed September 9, 2024).

5   New York State Division of Criminal Justice Services, "Crime in New York State: 2021 Final Data," *New York State Crime Report,* https://www.criminaljustice.ny.gov/crimnet/ojsa/Crime%20in%20NYS%202021.pdf (accessed September 9 2024).

charges of falsifying business records—which, in reality, were just thirty-four instances of the same supposed "crime," listed separately so the press could run with the inflated number. It was a Frankenstein case in every sense of the word, assembled of whatever crap Alvin Bragg and his squad could find laying around the office.

The case, which came to be called *New York v. Trump*, was the first of four Trump indictments to make it to a courtroom. From jury selection on April 15 all the way to the day President Trump was found guilty, I covered every detail of Alvin Bragg's nonsensical case against the former president creating a Trump-on-Trial special at noon every day. I spoke with legendary Harvard law professor Alan Dershowitz, Judge Andrew Napolitano, and several of President Trump's lawyers. All of them were shocked by what they were seeing. There were no cameras in the courtroom, and Juan Merchan, the judge in the case, often threw out journalists so he could work the case in secret.

"When he throws the journalists out," Alan Dershowitz (who was right there in the courtroom) told me, "his true self comes to the fore. He reminded me of the psycho from the movie *Taxi Driver*, who said, *You lookin' at me? You lookin' at me?* He said to the witness's lawyer, '…If you ever look at me again, if you ever bat your eyes again, I will strike all your testimony.…' The idea that the judge would strike testimony from the defense because he didn't like the way the witness *looked* at him? I've never seen such a thing. I've been in courtrooms in China and Russia and Italy and Israel. I've never quite seen a judge acting that way."

It hearkened back to a few weeks earlier, when Judge Merchan had warned President Trump that he would impose a gag order because of a facial expression the former president had made during the testimony of the discredited porn actress Stormy Daniels. To me, it seemed totally unreasonable to ask anyone—let alone a former president being falsely accused of horrible things in a courtroom—*not* to make a face, or at least do the occasional eyeroll. At the very least, it was hard not to seriously question the motivation of the prosecution as the ridiculous cast of characters took the stand week after week after week.

On the afternoon of the guilty verdict, it was clear that the fix was in. In the legacy press, no one cared that our country was quickly sliding into third-world, banana republic territory. The media were *giddy* to report that President Trump, the man who had exposed them for the liars and hacks that they all are, had been convicted of thirty-four felonies. They had been waiting to use the word *felon* to describe this man for years; and now their moment was here, like Christmas morning for those suffering from Trump derangement syndrome. It didn't matter that these felonies were nonsensical, as anyone who'd seen an episode of *Law & Order* would know. All the legacy press wanted was to be rid of President Trump.

While I was anchoring our live breaking coverage, President Trump emerged from the courtroom, looking both angry and disappointed and said "This was a disgrace. This was a rigged trial by a conflicted judge who was corrupt." He said he'd keep fighting for the country and Constitution and that the real verdict would happen on November 5 by the people. I tossed to our reporters, who were covering the protests outside the courtroom. Many people were on the streets, chanting in support of President Trump. It was good to see that not everyone had been brainwashed! It felt good to know that although lawfare was alive and well, the American people were not going to simply tolerate or accept it. We heard testimony from people on the streets who believed the verdict was a travesty. During his own press conference a short time later, DA Alvin Bragg didn't get a single question about the two-tiered justice system he'd instituted. He wasn't asked about the dangerous precedent he was setting by weaponizing the legal system in the way he had. All he could say was that he had "done his job."

I left the studio that night fighting off waves of anger and sadness. Real Americans, I knew, didn't believe anything that had been said in the courtroom. Even with the absence of cameras or good reporting, even with President Trump under a ridiculous gag order, they knew that the conviction was nothing more than a political hit job—just like the other three trials the former president was facing. Up to the moment before the verdict was read, I had still believed that there might be a mistrial or an acquittal. But then I received the news of the verdict in my email. Although he was convicted, it's likely he'll win on appeal, especially seeing how unfairly Judge Merchan behaved during the trial. That didn't matter to the Trump-hating Left; they wanted the verdict for the label, for the talking point. They assumed that Americans would be too disengaged to look beyond the headlines. This miscalculation of the electorate is a mistake the Left makes at their own peril.

The United States had entered another new political era—one in which the current president's party could prosecute its political rivals without even a hint of pushback from the legacy press. One in which the man in the White House, obviously functioning without all his mental faculties, would receive cover from those same media institutions because in their eyes, he was better than President Trump. The thought alone made me sick.

After reporting live, wall-to-wall, on the verdict, I had a flight to catch to Boston. Leaving Palm Beach International, the flight path took the plane directly over Mar-a-Lago, which glistened beside the Atlantic Ocean. On the night of this historic verdict, I reflected on the other unprecedented attack on President Trump when the FBI raided his private residence there, shattering yet another norm of the US political system.

As my plane headed north over the Atlantic, the "classified documents" case against President Trump was working its way through the court of Judge Aileen Cannon, who would eventually dismiss it on the grounds that Jack Smith, the special prosecutor, was illegally appointed to his role by the attorney general. Of course, we didn't know this yet. The cases against the president, as well as the total abdication of duty by the corporate press, had made things seem almost completely hopeless.

The United States of America seemed broken. For one night I pondered, *What do we wake up to tomorrow?*

The next day, the political landscape had shifted 180 degrees.

Early reports suggested that the Trump campaign had set fundraising records in the twenty-four hours since the verdict had been announced. Footage of real Americans on the street suggested that all was not lost. People were predicting a red wave in November. T-shirts and hats with President Trump's mugshot—the picture that the Left and the legacy media thought was going to sink his campaign—began popping up all over the place.

In early June, President Trump joined TikTok at a UFC match and got a million followers almost immediately. The fundraising totals just forty-eight hours after the New York verdict came down topped $200 million. When President Trump walked into the crowd at a UFC fight, he received a wild standing ovation that lasted for minutes. Outside the courtroom and the liberal media's echo chamber, the image of President Trump was untarnished. If anything, it was stronger than it had ever been.

The Biden campaign—soon to be the who-the-hell-knows campaign—knew this, which was why it had to step up its attacks to levels that would have been unthinkable just a few months earlier. On May 31, Alex Soros—the son of George Soros—tweeted: "Democrats should refer to Trump as a convicted felon at every opportunity. Repetition is the key to a successful message and we want people to wrestle with the notion of hiring a convicted felon for the most important job in the country!" Joe Biden (or whoever was typing messages for him at the time) issued a statement that attempted to pin the "felon" label on President Trump. The statement failed to mention that it was Matthew Colangelo, the number-three person at the Biden Justice Department, who had previously investigated Trump and, now, abruptly left his high-ranking federal job to work as counsel on the Alvin Bragg team in its persecution of the former president. That, I guess, would have made the blatant election interference a little too obvious, even for Team Biden.

On June 4, before the infamous debate, Trump's senior advisor Jason Miller joined me on *Newsline*. He said, "It's all weaponized. They can't run on any of the core issues. And quite frankly, that's why President Trump's numbers keep going up.... Americans are suffering all around the country. They're having real problems. They're having to decide between groceries or gas, are they able to do a vacation this year. People are having to pick up second jobs and cash out 401(k)s to make ends meet."

It was no wonder Democrats had to step up the rhetoric. Their worst, break-glass-in-case-of-emergency strategy against President Trump hadn't worked. Even in the face of a phony felony conviction, Trump continued to rise in the polls. All they could do was fall back on the old reliable trick of calling him a fascist, telling the American people that he was a "danger to democracy." And even when that rhetoric led to the attempted assassination of a presidential candidate in July 2024, they didn't stop. For weeks after Trump was almost killed by an assassin's bullet, MSNBC's Joy Reid continued to suggest that the entire event had been staged. Speaking from her home, she said, "We still don't know for sure whether Donald Trump was hit by a bullet. We know almost nothing." Later, on television, she suggested that President Trump surviving a bullet to the ear was the same as Joe Biden remaining alive after catching COVID-19. What is wrong with these depraved pundits? Apparently plenty. Reports said that NBC bosses were so concerned about Joe Scarborough, Mika Brzezinski, and their guests' potential inappropriate commentary that they took *Morning Joe* off the air the Monday after the assassination attempt.

In the middle of June, it was revealed that *Time* magazine, once known as a straight-down-the-middle publication, decided not to use the now-famous photograph of President Trump raising his fist to the crowd. The reason, according to a leaked comment from the magazine's photo editor, was that the photo made the former (and probably future) president "look too good." Oh, OK. So the reality of what happened should be suppressed because of the media's bias. Clearly, there was nothing that the establishment wouldn't do to keep Donald Trump from winning the White House again. They would bury stories, cover up lies, and weaponize the justice system if it meant they'd have some chance of taking down Donald Trump.

Amazingly, throughout all the post-shooting chaos, Joe Biden insisted that he would continue his campaign for the presidency. During his attempted bounce-back interview with George Stephanopoulos, he said that the only way he'd quit was if "the Lord Almighty" came down and told him he was going to lose to Donald Trump.

Now, I'm not sure whether the Lord actually did come down to tell Joe Biden his time was up. I seriously doubt it.

What I *do* know is that God showed up during the summer of 2024, when things seemed more uncertain than they'd been since at least the late 1960s. But He didn't go to the Delaware beach house where Joe Biden was, once again, hiding from the world in his basement instead of campaigning. He went straight to Milwaukee, where I and a few thousand other conservative Americans gathered to celebrate the miraculous survival of President Trump.

And if you doubt that it really was a miracle, go ahead and turn the page.

CHAPTER NINE

BY THE GRACE OF GOD

I've seen some amazing crowds in my life.

In 1985, my mom scored me and a couple of friends tickets (and backstage passes) to see Prince in Worcester, Massachusetts, on the Purple Rain tour. I still have a memory of standing in the crowd with my lace fingerless gloves on, thinking my mom was the absolute coolest for getting us into the arena. As Prince took the stage and spoke the intro to "Let's Go Crazy" ("Dearly beloved, we are gathered here today to get through this thing called *life*..."), thousands of people just like me went nuts. The rafters shook from the weight of all the jumping and shuffling feet.

Almost forty years later, I stood in the Fiserv Forum in Milwaukee, Wisconsin, watching the country singer Lee Greenwood take the stage. It was Monday, July 15, 2024, and the Republican National Convention was about to begin. As the piano played the first chords of his immortal anthem "God Bless the USA," Greenwood launched into a speech introducing President Trump, who, less than forty-eight hours earlier, had survived an attempt on his life.

"Prayer works!" Greenwood said. "This nation, based on faith. Prayer works because he was sure, as Donald Trump turned his head just slightly, that the bullet missed him just enough to save his life to be the next President of the United States."

The "voice of God" (which, as it turns out, is what people in the entertainment business call the booming voice that comes over the loudspeaker in arenas) announced President Trump, and the crowd went nuts. Lee Greenwood began his anthem, and the cheers grew louder.

The next day when he joined me in the Newsmax booth at the arena on *Newsline*, he described what it was like being part of that historic moment and said that his words came "straight from the heart." That entire week, I reported live from the RNC, covering history in real time. It was an amazing experience!

Compared to the powerful reception President Trump got that evening in Milwaukee, the roar of all those Prince fans was nothing. Finally, after days of waiting, here was concrete proof that President Trump was alive and well. Wearing a bandage on his ear and a solemn, contemplative look on his face he emerged from backstage, slowly walking out to wave to the packed floor of delegates before joining his family in their seats. I was fortunate to see this breathtaking moment with my own eyes while anchoring our nighttime coverage with my colleagues from our Newsmax booth. There he was, standing in front of us, I do believe saved by a miracle. In that moment I don't know if the nation felt closer to God, but I know that I did.

Watching it all unfold, I thought of the Bible scripture in Paul's letter to the Ephesians: "Put on the full armor of God, so that you can take your stand against the devil's schemes."

President Trump had certainly been wearing the armor of God on the evening of July 13, 2024, when he managed to narrowly avoid the bullet of an assassin. Thanks to that armor (and no thanks to the Secret Service), he managed to escape with his life. For the next few days, this verse would be quoted often, largely because the Ephesians verse, 6:11, is also the exact time that President Trump was shot in Butler,

Pennsylvania. But his near death was a grim reminder that in Joe Biden's America, we were all less safe. Even presidential candidates couldn't be kept safe from the rampant lawlessness and lack of accountability that now defined our everyday lives.

Tomorrow is never promised. As a Christian, I try to live every day with this knowledge. But watching someone almost have his life taken from him before all our eyes reinforced the idea for me. And I wasn't the only one. Walking around the Republican National Convention in Milwaukee, where thousands of donors, delegates, and journalists had gathered to formally nominate Donald Trump and J.D. Vance for the Republican ticket, I heard God mentioned more times than I could count. No one could believe just how close the country had come to utter chaos, or how tragic it was that Corey Comperatore, a husband, father, and volunteer firefighter, had been killed by a bullet that was meant for the former president. He died a hero, his widow said, shielding his family with his body. His last words were "get down."

Because of what we all witnessed, the speakers were not hesitant to talk about God. Even the ones who weren't pastors (or even Christians) spoke about miracles and divine intervention. Senator Tim Scott gave one of the most electrifying speeches of the night, saying, "The devil came to Pennsylvania holding a rifle, but the American lion got back on his feet."

On the first day of the convention, I ran into Russell Brand, the British actor and comedian who, a few months earlier, had announced his conversion to Christianity. As soon as I saw him enter the hall, I went up to him and told him that I, too, was a Christian, and that I was so happy to hear he'd recently become a follower of Jesus. His eyes lit up. As we walked together through a set of double doors, he was instantly recognized by a group of journalists, all hungry for an interview. But he was unfazed. Rather than giving in to the questions being shouted in his direction, he kept his eyes locked on me and said he'd be happy to have a discussion about the Lord. His assistant took down my number, and he disappeared into the crowd.

I loved Brand in *Forgetting Sarah Marshall*, but if you told me back then that he and I would sit down someday for a conversation about God, I probably would have laughed at you. Modern society, especially Hollywood, has been moving in an inexorably satanic direction for some time. Marriage rates are plummeting. So is the rate of church attendance. More young people are identifying as atheists, and fewer than ever are espousing the Christian values me and my friends had been raised with. By the early 2020s, you only had to flip on the television or open Instagram to see evidence of the rot that was beginning to pervade our society.

How else could you explain someone like singer Sam Smith, who pranced around the stage of the Grammy Awards in February 2023, his pale fat spilling from his leather pants, singing about the devil and promoting the trans agenda? Watching *that*, as well as covering many other troubling stories—after-school clubs in Iowa sponsored by the Church of Satan, for instance—I don't know how anyone could deny that the United States of America (and the world, for that matter) is in the midst of a serious spiritual battle. This would become crystal clear at the end of July 2024, when the opening ceremony of the Olympic Games in Paris presented a clear mockery of Leonardo da Vinci's "The Last Supper," with transsexuals and naked weirdos painted head to toe in blue standing in for Jesus' disciples. It was a disgusting display of just how far our society has been allowed to rot.

Thankfully we have people who are willing to fight back. At the RNC in Milwaukee, I saw many of them. As the week went on, I conducted some truly memorable interviews. One night, I spoke with Senator Ron Johnson, who let me know that he was the one who gave President Trump the chart on illegal immigration that ended up saving his life: "We gave it to him on the plane," he said, referring to a flight to a previous rally. "He used it that day, and he's been using it ever since. President Trump turned to point to that chart at the Butler, PA, rally, and he's literally crediting the chart with saving his life! God works in mysterious ways."

"Yes," I said. "And His plan is better than our plan."

On July 18, I interviewed Trump senior advisor Jason Miller, who previewed the amazing lineup of speakers at the RNC. In the middle of the interview, I broke the news live on air that former President Barack Obama had privately told allies that Joe Biden seriously needed to consider his viability for reelection. As Jason Miller put it, "This makes it official. They're not even stabbing Joe Biden in the back; they're stabbing him in the chest. This is a political coup. And with this chaos going on…the question is: *Who is running the country?*"

For the next few days, we got no answer. But we *were* reminded of what real leadership looks like. What struck me most about the speakers at the RNC was their willingness to put their Judeo-Christian faith front and center. Unlike the Democrats, who in the lead-up to the 2020 election *removed* the word "God" from the Pledge of Allegiance during their convention, Republicans were not afraid to speak about the divine. And how could they avoid it, given the events of the preceding few days? Anyone who was there with me in the Fiserv Forum that week will testify that there was a presence in the arena. As Trump's Secretary of Housing and Urban Development Ben Carson put it during his speech, "God lowered a protective shield around the former president." During the benediction for the event, Pastor James Roemke got up in front of the crowd and did a killer Trump impression, holding up his hands and saying, "You're gonna be so blessed! You're gonna be tired of being blessed. I guarantee it!"

The crowd erupted in laughter and cheers.

At the RNC, I began to feel extremely optimistic about the future of the United States, which wasn't easy at the time. Being around that many patriotic people was proof that even with all the lawfare being waged by the Biden-Harris administration, and even with the corporate press continuing to twist the truth, good can still prevail over evil.

It might seem hyperbolic to frame an upcoming election as a battle between good and evil, but I've been reporting on our political divide for years, and seeing the direction in which the country has been moving, I don't know what else to call it. As a Christian, I know evil when I see it.

This administration endorses the mutilation of children in the name of gender ideology, prioritizes radical trans rights over the safety and dignity of women and girls, and sanitizes the murder of innocent lives as mere reproductive health care. They've opened our borders, allowing millions of unvetted immigrants in, and are providing them with services that US citizens don't receive. They have shown us that, for some reason, they don't care about the people they swore to protect and serve. These actions represent not just policy disagreements but a direct assault on the very moral fabric that upholds our civilization. We are witnessing the unraveling of core principles that have sustained humanity for centuries, and the stakes have never been higher. This election is about choosing between preserving the values that define our humanity or succumbing to an agenda that threatens to destroy them.

It is, quite literally a battle between good and evil.

And it requires all of us on the side of good to dig deep and remember what *good* really means.

I grew up with a mother who was a devout Catholic. Almost every Sunday, she would come in my room and rouse me from sleep, telling me it was time to get in the car and head to Arch Street in Boston. We always went to The Shrine of St. Anthony, a beautiful church that was my mother's favorite near the Downtown Crossing T stop in the middle of the city.

There were two floors in the shrine. When it was full, which it usually was around Easter and Christmas, hundreds of parishioners packed into both sanctuaries, singing hymns and reciting prayers.

There were parts of Mass I liked—the hymns and communion.

As a kid, I wasn't crazy about going to church, but it was important to my mom and she always made Sundays special.

After Mass, we would often go out to a diner to eat and sometimes go shopping at the legendary original Filene's Basement. I loved shopping with Mom as she had a great eye and could always find a true bargain. My mom mastered the whole high-low vibe. She loved a deal, and she would mix sale items with her special Bonwit Teller and Neiman Marcus investment pieces that also filled her closet.

To this day, the sound of an organ stirs something in the back of my mind that says, *Go in peace and enjoy your bargain hunting!* When my mother was away on work trips, she'd still require that I go to Mass on my own to the local church within walking distance of our house. When she got home, she'd ask me to present the weekly bulletin as proof that I'd attended the entire Mass. She wanted receipts!

Looking back, I'm grateful that her faith was strong even if it took me some time to get close to God. My mom was an amazing role model. In fact, she could not have been better, especially in showing me the importance of building a spiritual life. We prayed often at home and it was comforting as a child to recite the Our Father and Hail Mary before bed. From the cross on the wall, to the Infant of Prague on my nightstand, my mother filled our home with religious objects.

As I grew older, I learned just how important faith was to my mother. One afternoon, almost out of the blue, she let me know that she'd considered becoming a nun when she was a young girl. Looking at her in her beautiful clothes and her honey blond hair, I could hardly imagine her hidden under a habit. I wondered if she was just kidding around. But as we discussed it, I learned that she'd been totally serious. To her, a life spent serving the Lord would have been a life well-spent. In the end, it was *her* mother who put a stop to the whole nun thing, forcing my mom to go out and get a job, which led to her meeting my father, and then to having me. I was blessed that she raised me with the beautiful Christian principles that she lived by.

When my mother died in February 2016, I delivered her eulogy. I talked about how my mom had put her personal life on hold to raise me, and how she'd taken me on many trips to see the world. I talked about her generosity and her beauty. She was physically beautiful, but her inner beauty was what made her so special. She sacrificed to give me a wonderful life, and she treated everyone with love and kindness. After she died, I found a stack of letters that people wrote to the airline she'd worked for praising her and thanking her for going above and beyond. Even legendary entertainer Bob Hope wrote her a thank you letter! More than once I saw her secretly pick up restaurant tabs of people in uniform because it was her way of thanking them for their service. She was kind and pure and led by the Spirit.

As an adult, I didn't go to church as much without my mom pushing me to accompany her. With my career, and a daughter of my own to raise, attending church was mostly centered on holidays and special occasions, and visits from my mom. But I never had a real crisis of faith until early 2002, when I began covering a scandal that was still unfolding in

Boston: one involving priests, children, and decades of lies and cover-ups.

In the beginning, I reported on the sexual abuse scandal of the Catholic Church the way everyone did. When there was a press conference, I would show up with the other reporters at lawyers' offices where they would recount stories of terrible sexual abuse by priests. Then the day would end with me doing a live news report outside the archdiocese building. And the next day it started all over again. This was a Catholic Church scandal of epic proportions. I couldn't imagine the pain that the parents of these victims, many of whom had been abused for decades, had felt. I couldn't imagine what it must have been like to know that the priest who abused you was still in his position, simply being shuffled around to different churches where he'd be able to hurt more kids.

One day, I got word that Cardinal Bernard Law, the head of the Catholic Church in Boston, was going to be reassigned. I wasn't surprised. Ever since the first stories about the sex abuse scandal began appearing in *The Boston Globe*, Cardinal Law's name had been mentioned over and over. For almost twenty years, he had ignored or covered up allegations of abuse in his parish, transferring priests who'd preyed on children rather than turning those priests over to the authorities. One priest under his supervision, John Geoghan, would later be found to have raped or molested more than one hundred young boys. As this scandal was rapidly unfolding, my local station dispatched me to Italy, where I would cover this international story from a Boston perspective.

Reporting on the story in Vatican City with my cameraman, the beauty of St Peter's Basilica was not enough to distract from the ugly and horrific details of the pedophilia by priests, and the Church's coverup. There were more press conferences, only now the press conferences were held in ancient rooms outfitted with priceless art and all manner of Catholic regalia. I felt no sense of awe in these rooms, only disgust. Of course, being a reporter on assignment, I ended up chasing some guy down a sidewalk, screaming questions at him and holding out my microphone, hoping to get a comment. Only now, that man was Cardinal Bernard Law, and by the time I saw him, he'd had a head start so there was no catching him. My cameraman got the shot of him being ushered into a waiting car by representatives of the Catholic Church, never to be heard from again.

At age twenty-seven, I was covering this global scandal that took down many in the Catholic Church. There was no bigger story. It's easy to call it a career defining moment, but personally it damaged me in ways I didn't understand at the time. My faith was shaken to my soul. Because of this, I stopped going to church almost entirely. In my mind, the Catholic Church was synonymous with this dark crime.

Then in 2018, when I was living in Los Angeles, of all places, something inside me changed. God got my attention. I happened to be living right next door to a church, very different from the ones I'd gone to with my mother as a young girl. This one, called Mosaic, sat on the busy corner of Hollywood Boulevard and La Brea, and it had a billboard right above it to advertise services. The people who flooded in on Sunday or the Wednesday service all had the LA, laid-back, California-cool look: jeans and long flowy dresses, tattoos and piercings. Justin Bieber and his glamorous wife Hailey would pop in some weeks, and even the show-biz-adjacent attendees would fawn over them.

I'm not sure what brought me in for the first time. Curiosity, mostly. But I do know that when I left, they handed me a free small bible. That sealed the deal. I was reminded that my relationship with God had nothing to do with priests or churches. It was about my relationship with Him. Getting close and staying close meant reading His word, and the way

I applied that word to my own life. In LA, I began reading a Bible verse every day, and I encouraged my daughter to join me. I was reminded that God can work miracles. His son Jesus died for our sins to give us eternal life. I got back to seeing for myself why the Bible is called "the living word." No matter what is going on in your life, you can pick it up, and it will speak to you. Now every day, I get an alert on my phone with a Bible verse, and it's usually exactly what I need in that moment. I'm not sure how I let so much time pass without God in my life. Now, a day doesn't go by without me acknowledging my Heavenly Father. When I open my eyes in the morning, I thank Him and I communicate with Him all throughout the day. We are in communion.

Without the presence of God in my life, I don't know where I would be. And I'm not alone. Lately, we've seen many people who walked away from the church—or, in some cases, were actively hostile to it—come back and realize just how important a strong sense of faith can be. I've already mentioned Russell Brand, whose amazing conversion to Christianity made headlines all over the world. There's also Ayaan Hirsi Ali, a Somali woman who was raised under an Islamic dictatorship called the Muslim Brotherhood, and who is now a fellow at the Hoover Institution. For years, Hirsi Ali was an atheist, believing that the only response to the horrible things she'd endured under Islam was to swear off all religions, Christianity included.

It wasn't until November 2023, just before the holiday season, that she had a conversion experience. Looking around at the state of the world, she saw what happens when people abandon faith. She saw, as she put it in her Christmas Day essay for UnHerd, "three different but related forces: the resurgence of great-power authoritarianism and expansionism in the forms of the Chinese Communist Party and Vladimir Putin's Russia; the rise of global Islamism, which threatens to mobilise a vast population against the West; and the viral spread of woke ideology which is eating into the moral fibre of the next generation."[1]

So, she came to embrace "the legacy of the Judeo-Christian tradition," which consists of "an elaborate set of ideas and institutions designed to safeguard human life, freedom and dignity—from the nation state and the rule of law to the institutions of science, health, and learning."

Over the past few years, the fact that our Founding Fathers built this nation on a foundation of faith has come under attack. Even the ideas set forth in the Declaration of Independence show how the founders believed in the divinity of Jesus and the wisdom of His teachings. You simply cannot separate one from the other.

From the beginning, God has been here in America. George Washington said, "to the distinguished character of Patriot, it should be our highest glory to add the more distinguished character of Christian." John Adams, who followed, him, dreamed in his private writings of a nation where every citizen would regulate their conduct by the Bible, creating a society grounded in justice, kindness, and reverence toward God. Thomas Jefferson knew that the liberties he wrote about in the Declaration of Independence could only be secure when rooted in the belief that they are a gift from God. This deep connection between faith and freedom was not merely philosophical but a guiding principle in the creation of our nation's laws and institutions.

Throughout history, presidents of the United States have turned to prayer in times of trouble. One of Ronald Reagan's favorite images, according to Lee Edwards of the Heritage

---

1   Ayaan Hirsi Ali, "Why I am now a Christian: Atheism can't equip us for civilizational war," UnHerd, December 25, 2023, https://unherd.com/2023/12/why-i-am-now-a-christian-2/ (accessed September 9, 2024).

Foundation, "was that of Gen. George Washington kneeling in the snow at Valley Forge, when the American cause seemed hopeless. That image, Reagan said, 'personified a people who knew it was not enough to depend on their own courage and goodness; they must also seek help from God, their Father and their Preserver.'"[2] Abraham Lincoln ended the Emancipation Proclamation with "I invoke the considerate judgment of mankind, and the gracious favor of Almighty God."

This continued all the way from Teddy Roosevelt to Franklin Delano Roosevelt up to George W. Bush, who often hosted religious leaders at the White House. The National Prayer Breakfast, which began in 1953, is another example of our nation's deep commitment to faith and the belief in a higher power guiding our leaders. This annual event brings together people from across the political spectrum to unite in prayer, reflecting on the enduring influence of Christian values on American public life. It serves as a reminder that, even in times of division, the nation's leaders recognize the importance of seeking divine guidance in their decisions.

For a while, we lost this.

But the tide is turning. I can feel it.

Every day, it seems more people are returning to Christianity. Even as misguided young people on college campuses embrace the replacement religion of wokeness, which allows them to do horrible things in the name of social justice, thousands more kids embrace more traditional values. Early in 2023, I was inspired by the story on the campus of Asbury University in Kentucky, where students held a chapel service that ended up lasting for weeks. In what became known as the "Asbury Revival," students sang songs and led prayers for

2   Lee Edwards, "Presidential Prayers: Turning to God in Times of Need," Heritage Foundation, April 6, 2020, https://www.heritage.org/religious-liberty/commentary/presidential-prayers-turning-god-times-need (accessed September 9, 2024).

hours on end, attracting other college students from all over the country.

As Sarah Thomas Baldwin, a professor at Asbury University, wrote in *Generation Awakened*, her book about the event, "What started as college students experiencing a fresh move of the Holy Spirit on Asbury's campus spontaneously combusted into a move of God upon the world. The bonfire of God's love burned on Asbury's campus for Generation Z, and the rest of us lit the wick of our hearts to the flame of the spirit."

Lately, we've seen many more examples of God in popular culture. One film in particular, called *Jesus Revolution*, tells the true story of the pastor Greg Laurie, who invited hippies to join his congregation to raise membership numbers in the 1970s. Shortly after the film's release, I asked Greg Laurie to come on my show to talk about the amazing religious revival he experienced in the 1970s and its relevance to current events.

"Art imitates life," he said. "Life is happening. We were trying to have this film made five years ago...and COVID hit. Then finally we got it done, and the timing could not be more perfect. God is at work. Are we seeing the beginning of another spiritual revival among young people? One thing you can't deny is that there is an awakening among college students."

Clearly, all is not lost in this country. Even the members of Gen Z—who, as we saw in Chapter Two, have some serious problems—are coming to see the value of a life lived in Christ.

Now, in many circles it's cool to be spiritual. Brilyn Hollyhand, an eighteen-year-old frequent guest of mine on *Newsline* and chairman of the Youth Advisory Council for the Republican National Committee, joined me during the convention to talk about his work. You'd never know he was nervous, but in his book *One Generation Away: Why Now Is the Time to Restore American Freedom*, he writes about how whenever he is nervous before making a public appearance or speech, he prays and gives it all to the Lord.

"My coping method is simple," he writes. "I give it all to the Lord. I put my full trust in Him. Before every big meeting, every interview, every speech, and every TV appearance, I recite a phrase aloud to myself: 'God, if it's your will, let it be done.' Why? Uttering those nine words is verbally surrendering all nerves, all anxiety, and all worry to God. If it is His will for this interview, speech, or TV hit to go well, I'm putting my full faith in Him for that to happen."

When I interviewed Brilyn at the RNC, God must have been with him. He knocked it out of the park in Milwaukee.

Everyone did!

In many ways, the RNC was exactly the opposite of the White House Correspondents' Dinner that I had attended a few weeks earlier. Rather than lying about the mental condition of Joe Biden—who, at the time, was still clinging to power, attempting to rally the delegates to earn the nomination of his party—Republicans pointed out the obvious about Biden. Rather than pretending inflation wasn't real, they called it out. Rather than making excuses for rising crime rates, they discussed what we should do about them. The same went for our open borders and the social decay we have all been seeing for the past four years.

After almost thirty years in journalism, I never thought I'd hear more true statements spoken at a party convention than at a dinner for members of the press. For years, I've believed that both political parties tend to lie to make themselves look good, and that it's the job of journalists to cut through the BS on both sides and get to the truth. But that model, like so much else, has broken down. Today, it's the Republican Party that is willing to speak the truth about what is happening in our country. The media, which has been entirely captured by the Democrat elite, no longer speaks for the American people.

They don't care about finding out what's true. They only care about pushing a left-wing agenda and protecting their favorite politicians.

The people who gathered in Milwaukee for the RNC, however, *did* care about the truth. That includes journalists, politicians, and voters. Speaking with people around the convention hall over the course of five days, I was reminded that in some places, people are still free to speak their minds and say what they believe. There was no censorship at the RNC that week. There were no talking points from high above that all speakers had to espouse. The mood was open and free. People of all races, ages, and belief systems gathered and went out after the official events were done for the day, many of them talking about how lucky they felt to be in that city at that very moment in time. I felt truly blessed to be sharing this good news on the air.

It was a direct contrast to the White House Correspondents' Dinner, where a mood of censoriousness and secrecy reigned. Looking back, I can see why. On the night of that dinner, the corporate press was keeping a big secret from the American people. Everyone in that room knew that Joe Biden was no longer fit for office, and they concealed it because they desperately wanted to stop President Trump from winning again. As the months went on, we saw them shift their story without ever stopping the barrage of lies and obfuscation. They told us that Donald Trump was a threat to democracy, and they told us that Kamala Harris was never the border czar. Then they told us that Weirdo Tim Walz was perfectly right to lie about his service in the Middle East. Clearly, these people have become nothing more than the PR arm of the Democratic Party.

When the Democrats say that hairy men with penises are women, they'll insert some scientific language into their stories, always from an "expert," that makes it sound true. When the Democrats say that Joe Biden, a man who was walking into walls in July 2024, is "the best he's ever been," the corporate press will bury all stories that express contrary facts, and shame anyone who tries to report the truth. As this book goes to press in the late summer of 2024, we are seeing this very process in action once again. Just a few weeks after President Trump announced that Senator J.D. Vance would become his vice-presidential nominee, almost every cable news program had some Democrat on who called him "weird." The Democrats loved it so much, in fact, that they made the man who coined the phrase *the vice-presidential nominee.*

Apparently, running with Walz's "weird" shtick was the best that the highly paid political consultants at the Democratic National Committee could come up with. It didn't seem to bother members of the Democratic Party—who, just days earlier, were telling us that drag queens should be allowed to read to children, and that biological men should be able to beat the crap out of women in Olympic boxing matches—had cozied up to plenty of weird people in the past.

And now he's running with the sleaziest, weirdest person of them all: Vice President Kamala Harris. For years, we've had a pretty conventional understanding of this country's first Jamaican, Indian, part-Canadian vice president who also happens to identify as a woman. Despite the media's attempt to convince us that anyone who has a problem with Harris must be racist or sexist, anyone who looks at her record for more than ten seconds can see that she is deeply unpopular because she has been *terrible* at every job she's ever held. Are we really supposed to believe that this daughter of college professors who, at one point, dated Montel Williams and the powerful California politician Willie Brown, got everything she has simply by being smart and working hard?

Please. No one likes her. But the Democratic Party is rallying around her anyway because it has no choice. And the media is going with it all, despite the fact that Harris seems hell-bent on speaking as little as possible to the corporate press. The coronation that occurred in the days after Joe Biden dropped out of the race was sickening. While President Trump made himself available to all kinds of audiences—even downright hostile ones—Kamala hid in the basement just like Joe did in 2020.

In journalism, you can't pretend there are two sides to every story. Sometimes there are fifty sides, and sometimes there is just one. And right now, the one side of the story about American politics is that we are engaged in a battle for this country—one that is about to come to a head as this book goes to print. On one side, we have people who don't like the United States of America at all, who want to poison the minds of our children with ideas about sex changes and socialism and the entirely fictional scourge of "systemic white supremacy" that supposedly plagues our institutions. For now, that side is led by Kamala Harris and Tim Walz. But who knows? By the time this book reaches your hands, the powers that be in the Democratic Party may have conducted another backroom, anti-democratic swap to install different candidates. Either way, those of us who still believe in freedom of speech, the freedom to worship, and life, liberty, and the pursuit of happiness will be up against a threat unlike anything we've ever faced.

On the other side—the *right* side—we have people who want to teach our children that this country is the greatest that has ever existed on planet earth. We have people who will strive to build amazing things and to end all the seemingly endless conflicts that have upended the globe over the past four years. These people, led by Donald Trump, don't want more foreign wars. They don't want the government or corporations shoving a woke agenda down our throats and making all dissent illegal. For the first time in my career as a journalist, I have come to realize that we are living through a moment in which, to coin a phrase, the right is *right*, and the other side is dead wrong. And, if you ask me, downright evil.

Over the course of the events described in this book—which have included a historic moment of reckoning on American campuses, a recusal on behalf of a sitting president, and the first attempted assassination of a presidential candidate since the 1980s—at times I have felt the country is in a downward spiral.

I rest in my faith. I steel myself for the events unfolding around us knowing God is in control and He is on our side.

As scripture tells us:

"If God is for us who can be against us?"
(Romans 8:31)

ABOUT THE AUTHOR

Bianca de la Garza is a ten-time Emmy® nominated, award-winning journalist who joined Newsmax in 2021 and currently is the solo host of *Newsline* and *Newswire*. She has spent over twenty years in news working for ABC and FOX television stations across the US covering major global news events. She began her career at the ABC Albany affiliate covering the politics of Governor George Pataki and Hillary Clinton, then reported on the Catholic Church's pedophilia scandal for FOX in both Boston and Rome. Bianca's award-winning reporting led to the closure by the feds of an illegal sweatshop in San Diego, California, along the Mexico border.

She received an Emmy® nomination for her coverage of the Royal Wedding of Prince William and Kate Middleton in London, UK. In addition, she was creator, host, and executive producer of *BIANCA*, a late-night show co-produced by SONY that aired in twenty million homes in the US on ABC and CBS television stations in 2015–2016, and was nominated for three Emmys.

The Latina is also an entrepreneur whose credits have been featured in *Forbes*, TheWrap, Business Insider, Deadline, *Inc.*, *Latina*, *Hola!* magazine, and *People en Español*.

Bianca is a proud single mom to her beautiful and talented daughter.

Made in the USA
Monee, IL
05 November 2024

69442786R00125